Henning Lühr

The World's Only International Kale Cookbook

50 recipes from 27 countries

Kellner Verlag
Bremen Boston

This book is registered with the German National Library.
The bibliographic data can be viewed online: **http://dnb.d-nb.de**.

Special Feature

Besides the myriad of recipes, the bilingual presentation of this book is unique: each recipe is in English as well as in its original language. This facilitates the communication between peoples from different countries and cultures.

Acknowledgements

The Bremen State Secretary of Finance Henning Lühr had the original idea for this book and subsequently, together with his many friends throughout the world, collected the recipes – in their respective languages. The translations into German for the first edition in 2011 were likewise a joint effort from multiple friends. Our heartfelt thanks to all, especially to Dr. Valentine-Thon for the current translation of the recipes into English.
We are grateful to the honorary citizen of Bremen Uwe Hollweg for his generous support of this book.

Kellner Publishing House
St.-Pauli-Deich 3 | D-28199 Bremen, Germany
Tel +49 421 77866 | Fax +49 421 704058
sachbuch@kellnerverlag.de | **www.kellnerverlag.de**
Translation into English: Dr. Elizabeth Valentine-Thon
Editing: Klaus Kellner
Layout: Manuel Dotzauer, Lisa Kranz
Cover: Designbüro Möhlenkamp & Schuldt, Bremen

The illustrations were contributed by:
(KH) Karin Hollweg (UR) Udo Reinfeld
(HL) Henning Lühr Klaus Kellner

Edition 2018 • ISBN 978-3-95651-197-4

Contents

4 **The World's Only International Kale Cookbook**
Henning Lühr

6 **Cooking with Kale – Tips for Its Purchase, Storage, and Use in Classical and International Kale Recipes**
Henning Lühr

8 **Recipes**
8 • Soups
18 • Salads
22 • Stews
36 • Casseroles
44 • Pesto and Marmalade
49 • Quiche, Cakes, and Pizza
54 • Crostini and Chips
56 • Kale with Meat and Seafood
68 • Fish and Kale
76 • Kale for Vegetarians
84 • Curry and Kale in Exotic Variations
88 • The Kale Classics from Northern Germany

94 **Kale Dishes Need Potatoes!**

98 **A Little Sausage Shop**

101 **America Discovers Kale**

103 **The Cabbage Tour – from a Meeting of Dignitaries to a Common People's Winter Entertainment**
Helga Bürster

105 **Bremen Offers More than Kale!**
Klaus Kellner

The World's Only International Kale Cookbook

The global player kale and Bremen

It is indeed remarkable that a »cabbage plant with a migrant background« has in Germany up until now been considered only a northern German vegetable with a long tradition. Especially in Bremen, a north German metropolitan city, with its centuries-old tradition of world trade, with the second largest harbor in Germany, with the world's largest Mercedes production and the famous Airbus and Space Industry, this was never disputed. This book will now surprise many:

Kale is an international vegetable, a culinary global player!

The international kale cuisine is characterized by a long tradition of typical dishes with their unique regional features. For several years now the international Crossover-Kitchen has been working with kale, combining it innovatively with oriental and Asian spices, various oils, exotic meat and fish recipes as well as with delicious desserts. Kale has even conquered America. Kale is hip and trendy.

In this unique international cookbook you will discover the magical world of kale recipes: soups, stews, salads, pesto, sandwich spreads, side dishes for fish, meat and sausages, as well as vegetarian delights. The result:

50 recipes from 27 countries. Enjoy your meal!

The remarkable career of a humble green vegetable

Before we set out on our thrilling search for clues to the origin of kale, let us review some basic information about this popular vegetable.

Kale, in Latin *Brassica oleracea*, belongs to the family of crucifers. It is a special form of cabbage, which like a palm – depending on the size of the plant – grows with long curly leaves that hang down. In the second year they develop large yellow flowers. After fertilization, pods with seeds develop. However, only the leaves are used for vegetable dishes.

Kale is also known regionally as curly kale, winter cabbage, collards, or savoy cabbage. In Switzerland it is called »Federkohl« or feathery cabbage. Brown kale, a Bremer specialty, is an unusual form of curly kale with brown colored leaves.

Kale has been, and still is, used not only as a vegetable. It is also considered to have medicinal properties for humans and animals. For example, in ancient Greece one believed that kale could combat the unpleasant effects of drunkenness. Hippocrates even recommended a broth of kale juice for coughs and hoarseness. In the Middle Ages and early Renaissance, kale was also used as decorative material for churches and celebrations.

Kale originated in the Mediterranean area, its exact place of origin discussed as either northern Africa or Greece. In the year 400 B. C. in Greece, a curly-leafed plant was described that later the Romans called Sabellian kale. The first clues to its presence in Northern Germany are found in contemporary accounts of the eating rituals and dishes of the Middle Ages. Typical growing regions for kale today are northern, middle, and western Europe, North and South America, East and West Africa, and South East Asia.

Cultural historians analyzed the history of kale only in conjunction with living conditions, dietary habits, and customs. We are entering »scientifically uncharted territory« when we refer to historical clues. Kale came originally from the Atlas mountain range in North Africa and provided the Berbers a decorative plant as well as livestock fodder. Around 800–900 A. D., the Vikings supposedly brought kale together with its roots from North Africa back to their homes during their raids and plunderings throughout the Mediterranean region. Necessity is the mother of invention: In the fateful year of 896 A.D., beetles destroyed the entire cabbage harvest in northern Europe – and with it the staple food of many people during the long winter months, besides herring, salted meat, and smoked sausages. In any case, the starving people saw that the kale brought by the Vikings was edible and gratefully consumed it.

But how did kale actually come to Germany?

The popularity of kale is certainly not due to imperialistic raids. The Vikings have to relinquish the honor of fathering kale in favor of migrant people bringing in their young plants. In the end it was illegal immigrants who established the long northern German kale tradition, as described in »historical novels«.

The »kale immigrants« originally came by ship from Ethiopia. Along the way they landed for several days each on Greece, Italy, Spain, Portugal, France, England, Belgium, and Holland, leaving several of their colleagues who then settled in the respective countries. Finally, the majority of the »kale immigrants« landed in Bremen, Germany, where they set up camp, reproduced, and became integrated settlers. Over the many years, their immigrant background was alluded to less and less frequently and at one point simply forgotten. As a result, the strong (but false!) belief that kale has always been an ancient German vegetable was firmly established.

Henning Lühr

Cooking with Kale – Tips for Its Purchase, Storage, and Use in Classical and International Kale Recipes

Purchase

Buy your kale at the vegetable market and, if you anticipate needing larger amounts, order it in advance. Kale is sold either as the whole plant – the famous northern German palm – or conveniently plucked apart. Always check that the kale has no yellow spots and, if you're buying the whole plant, check that the cut end is not dried out. If you don't have the time to buy fresh kale, you can go ahead and use the frozen variety without a bad conscience.

Storage

If you are using fresh kale, don't let it stand around too long. Its vitamins remain intact to a large degree during cooking, but they dissipate rapidly through storage in the vegetable bin. Yellow spots will also develop due to extended storage at home. You won't have these problems with frozen kale. On the other hand, you should not allow frozen kale to thaw before use, as the kale can easily then become sour.

Preparation

If you have bought the whole plant, you have to first detach the leaves from the stock and then remove the individual leaves. By pulling the leaves off, they retain their natural structure, so you should avoid cutting them off. Remove the tough leaf veins, as these will remain inedible even after extensive cooking. Fresh kale has to be washed thoroughly before cooking, as dirt can collect in the curly leaves. If you don't cook kale often, we suggest surveying your cupboards in advance and selecting the appropriate equipment. Without adequate preparation or experience, it is easy to get hectic in the kitchen, since in the end you want to serve everything on the table at the same time and piping hot.

Cooking hearty kale

For a hearty portion, we recommend about 500g fresh kale. Don't be intimidated by the huge volume of the kale – like spinach, kale collapses during cooking. Select a large pot with a heavy bottom. The heavy bottom allows for a good distribution of heat. For each portion of kale add one onion. Chop the onions into pieces (not too small) and braise them with lard in the pot until glazed. Add the kale slowly, since especially with the frozen variety, mixing can be difficult and the kale can easily burn. Add sufficient water so that the kale does not burn during the entire cooking time. We recommend adding a little salt at the start of cooking, but not too much, since at the end of the cooking time, very salty smoked-cured meat will be added to the kale according to taste. Allow the kale to simmer gently for at least two hours in a covered pot. Don't forget to stir the kale often – burnt kale smells disgusting. After two hours the kale should still be firm – or as the northern Germans say, al dente – it should still have a certain consistency. Now add smoked ham or bacon, cured pork, and one or two skinned Pinkel sausages to the kale. If you like, you can also add the rest of the Pinkel sausages to the pot, or you can warm these up in an extra pot to keep the kale from getting too fatty. You have to now lower the temperature even further, though stirring will get more difficult. After another half hour, depending on how much water is in the kale, you should add some ground barley to the pot, as these absorb some of the fluid. Cook the kale another good half hour and stir even more religiously – the addition of ground barley renders the kale even more susceptible to burning. When the kale has reached the desired consistency, taste it. Pepper and allspice especially can easily lose their normal taste from extensive cooking and develop an unpleasant spiciness. Definitely add some sugar; even in the classical Bremen recipe you need to add sugar. Sugar serves to counter kale's bitterness.

Serving hearty kale

We highly recommend preparing well how you want to serve the kale. Consider in advance which serving bowls and platters you have and which side dishes will be served. Not only the kale will be added to the serving dish but also the potatoes and meats such as ham, cured pork, and various Pinkel sausages. With adequate preparation, serving should be no problem. It's especially good if you warm the dishes up first, as lukewarm kale is not very tasty. Don't serve everything you have carefully prepared all at once, better is to serve hot portions as needed. The kale and sausages retain their heat in the pot for quite a while, but once served on the table, quickly get cold. A good kale meal requires a clear, well-cooled liquor. We recommend a simple grain-based one.

Preparing and serving other kale recipes from this cookbook

The huge array of international kale recipes in this book should be served according to the individual recipe, along with the respective recommendations for drinks. *Henning Lühr*

Soups

Kale cream soup

Ingredients

- 300 g kale
- 3 small onions
- 2 Tbsp pure sunflower oil
- 800 ml water
- 3 tsp powdered vegetable broth
- 500 g potatoes
- 6 Tbsp sweet cream
- 200 ml milk
- 3 slices of coarse rye bread
- 2 Tbsp sunflower oil

30 minutes

Recipe

1. Clean and wash kale, remove leaves from stem, and chop coarsely. Peel onions and chop into dices.
2. Heat 2 Tbsp sunflower oil in a pot and braise the onions until glassy. Add the kale and steam briefly.
3. Add water and dissolve the powdered vegetable broth in it. Bring to a boil, then lower the temperature and simmer for 5–7 minutes in the covered pot.
4. Wash, peel, and cut the potatoes into small pieces. Add to the soup and cook for further 10–12 minutes until the vegetable is soft. Puree the soup with a hand-held blender.
5. Mix in sweet cream and milk.
6. Remove the crust from the rye bread and cut into dices.
7. Heat 2 Tbsp sunflower oil in a frying pan. Roast the pieces of bread until crispy.
8. Serve the soup in bowls and garnish with the croutons.

Grünkohlcreme-suppe

Germany

Zutaten

- 300 g Grünkohl
- 3 kleine Zwiebeln
- 2 EL reines Sonnenblumenöl
- 800 ml Wasser
- 3 TL gekörnte Brühe
- 500 g Kartoffeln
- 6 EL Schlagsahne
- 200 ml Milch
- 3 Scheiben Bauernbrot
- 2 EL Sonnenblumenöl

30 Minuten

Zubereitung

1. Grünkohl putzen, waschen, Blätter von den Stielen entfernen und grob hacken. Zwiebeln schälen und in Würfel schneiden.
2. In einem Topf 2 EL Sonnenblumenöl heiß werden lassen und die Zwiebeln darin glasig dünsten. Den Grünkohl zugeben und kurz mitdünsten.
3. Wasser zugießen und gekörnte Brühe darin auflösen. Zum Kochen bringen und zugedeckt 5–7 Min. bei geringer Wärmezufuhr garen.
4. Kartoffeln waschen, schälen und in Würfel schneiden. Zur Suppe geben und weitere 10–12 Min. kochen, bis das Gemüse weich ist. Die Suppe mit dem Schneidestab pürieren.
5. Sahne und Milch unterrühren.
6. Vom Bauernbrot die Rinde entfernen und in Würfel schneiden.
7. In einer Pfanne 2 EL Sonnenblumenöl heiß werden lassen. Die Brotwürfel darin knusprig rösten.
8. Die Suppe auf Tellern anrichten und mit den Brotwürfeln garniert servieren.

Portuguese kale soup

Ingredients

- 200 g beans, dried, small, white, soaked overnight
- 2 onions, large, diced
- 500 g kale, chopped
- 200 g potatoes, peeled and diced
- 2 tomatoes, diced
- 1 tsp vinegar
- 4 cloves of garlic, pressed
- 200 g spicy sausage, diced, chorizo or cabanossi
- salt
- pepper, freshly ground

Recipe

1. Rinse the soaked beans in cold water.
2. Add 2.5 l water or unsalted vegetable broth to a large pot and heat it up. Add the beans, onions, kale, diced potatoes, diced tomatoes, vinegar, chorizo, and garlic.
3. Simmer for 2 hours at low heat, occasionally stirring. Add more water or broth as needed. When the soup is cooked, add salt and pepper.
4. Switch off the burner, cover the pot, and let the soup sit for 10 minutes before serving.

ca. 30 minutes

Portugal

Sopa portuguesa le couve

Ingredientes

- 200 g de feijões brancos secos e pequenos
- 2 cebolas grandes
- 500 g le couve
- 200 g de batatas descascadas e cortadas em quadradinhos
- 2 tomates
- 1 colher de chá de vinagre
- 4 dentes de alho amassados
- 200 g de paio cortado em cubos ou rodelas, substituir por chouriço ou por Kabanossi
- Sal
- Pimenta moída na hora

Cerca de 30 minutos

Modo de fazer

1. Deixar os feijões de molho em água fria durante a noite.
2. Juntar 2,5 l de água ou de caldo de carne sem sal. Cortar a cebola, a batata, o tomate e o paio em cubos, le couve e amassar o alho. Levar uma panela grande ao fogo com um pouco de óleo, fritar a cebola e o alho, juntar a batata, a couve e o paio. Colocar a colher de vinagre.
3. Deixe cozinhar por 2 horas em fogo lento. Mexer de vez em quando, para a sopa não grudar no fundo da panela. Se necessário, colocar mais água ou caldo de carne. Quando a sopa estiver pronta, temperar com sal e pimenta.
4. Desligar o fogo, tampar a panela e deixar descansar por 10 minutos antes de servir.

Swedish kale soup

Ingredients

- 350 g kale
- a pinch of salt
- a pinch of pepper
- 3 Tbsp butter (melted)
- 4 Tbsp flour
- 1.5 l vegetable broth
- 150 ml sweet cream
- 600 g bologna sausage
- 2.5 l salt water

25 minutes

Recipe

1. Wash the kale and remove the leaves.
2. Bring the salt water to boil in a large pot, add the kale leaves, and simmer for 10 minutes at medium temperature.
3. Remove the kale leaves from the water with a skimmer, drain well, and chop into fine pieces.
4. Heat the butter in a pot and sprinkle the flour over it. Sauté briefly and then add the broth.
5. Keep stirring until thickened. Add the finely chopped kale. Bring the soup to a boil and then let it simmer on low heat for about 5 minutes.
6. Cut the bologna sausage into dices, fry briefly, and then add to the soup.
7. Season to taste with salt, pepper, and sweet cream.

Svensk grönkålssoppa

Sweden

Ingredienser

- 750 g grönkål
- en nypa salt
- en nypa peppar
- 3 msk smält smör
- 4 msk vetemjöl
- 1,5 l grönsaksbuljong
- 150 ml grädde
- 600 g t.ex. falukorv i små bitar
- 2,5 l saltat vatten

25 min.

Så här lagar du soppa på grönkål

1. Använder du färsk grönkål så plockar du och sköljer bladen och rensar dem samtidigt. Repa kålbladen från stjälkarna.
2. Värm upp det saltade vattnet i en stor gryta tills det kokar. Lägg i grönkålsbladen och låt dem koka på medelvärme i 10 minuter.
3. Ta upp grönkålsbladen med en hålslev. Låt dem rinna av väl och skär dem i strimlor.
4. Värm upp smör i en gryta och tillsätt vetemjöl. Häll sedan på grönsaksbuljong.
5. Rör ordentligt tills såsen blir krämig.
   Lägg nu i den finstrimlade grönkålen. Koka upp grönkålsoppan och låt den dra i ytterligare 5 minuter på lägre värme.
6. Skär nu falukorv i små bitar. Stek den några minuter och lägg korven i grönkålsoppan.
7. Smaka av grönkålsoppan med salt, peppar och grädde.

Finnish vegetable soup kesä

Ingredients:

- 2 medium-sized new potatoes
- 200 g snow peas
- 6 small carrots
- 200 g fresh kale
- 1 small cauliflower
- 200 g green beans
- 50 ml sweet cream
- 1 egg yolk, 2 Tbsp flour
- 20 g butter
- milk
- 200 g shrimps (thawed or fresh)
- salt
- white pepper
- dill or parsley

40 minutes

Recipe

1. Clean and wash the vegetables, cut into equal-sized dices. First cook the carrots for 5 minutes, then add the other vegetables and cook for 5 more minutes.
2. In a separate pot prepare a sauce from butter and flour and, while constantly stirring, add the vegetable broth (after passing through a sieve) and about 2 Tbsp of milk. Mix well.
3. Whisk the egg yolk and sweet cream together in a bowl and then add by the spoonful about 100 ml of the hot vegetable broth.
4. Pour everything back into the pot and stir again well. Then add the vegetables to the soup and heat again.
5. Just before boiling add the shrimps.
6. After 3–4 minutes you can season to taste and then serve with the chopped herbs.

Kesäkeitto

Finland

Tarvikkeet

- 2 keskikokoista uutta perunaa
- 200 g (sokeri)herneitä
- 6 pientä porkkanaa
- 200 g tuoretta lehtikaalia
- 1 pieni kukkakaali
- 200 g vihreitä papuja
- 50 ml kermaa
- 1 munankeltuainen, 2 rkl jauhoja
- 20 g voita
- maitoa
- 200 g katkarapuja (sulatetuja tai tuoreita)
- suolaa
- valkopippuria
- tilliä tai persiljaa

Valmistus

1. Puhdista vihannekset, paloittele ne samankokoisiksi kuutioiksi. Keitä ensin porkkanoita 5 min., lisää muut vihannekset ja keitä vielä 5 min.
2. Valmista toisessa kattilassa vositа ja jauhoista valkoinen suurus, lisää siihen kokoajan hämmentäen vihannesten keitinvettä sekä n. 2 rkl maitoa. Sekoita hyvin.
3. Sekoita munankeltuainen ja kerma kulhossa, lisää siihen lusikoittain n. 100 ml kuumaa keitinvettä.
4. Kaada seos kattilaan, sekoita kaikki perusteellisesti. Lisää vihannekset ja kuumenna.
5. Lisää katkaravut hieman ennen kiehumista.
6. Kiehauta keittoa 3–4 min, mausta ja tarjoile silputun tillin tai persiljan kanssa.

Turkish kale soup

Ingredients

- 1/2 cup dried beans
- 3 tsp salt
- 2 cups corn
- 3 tsp black pepper
- 5 cups water
- 3/4 tsp red pepper
- 2 onions
- 5 Tbsp ground beef
- 2 Tbsp butter or margarine
- 2 tsp tomato paste
- 10 leaves of kale

70 minutes

Recipe

1. Soak the beans and corn overnight in 2 cups of water.
2. Cook the beans and corn in a pot for 45–50 minutes.
3. Braise the chopped onions and ground beef in margarine for 10 minutes in a large pot, then mix in the tomato paste and heat up.
4. Add the kale, beans and corn and cook for about 20 minutes.
5. Season to taste just before serving.

Karalahana çorbas

Turkey

Malzemeler

- Yarım fincan kuru fasulye
- 3 çay kaşığı tuz
- 2 fıncan mısır tanesi
- 3 çay kaşıgı karabiber
- 5 fincan su
- 3/4 çay kaşığı kırmızı renkli karabiber
- 2 sogan
- 5 yemek kaşığı kıyma
- 2 yemek kaşığı tereyağı veya margarin
- 2 çay kaşığı salca
- 10 yaprak karalahana

Hazırlanışı

1. Fasulye ve mısırı geceden 2 fincan suya koyup sabaha kadar bekletin.
2. Ertesti gün fasulye ve mısırı asağı yukarı 45–50 dakika suda pişirin.
3. Büyük bir tencerede doğranmıs soğanları ve kıymayı margarinle 10 dakika kavurun. Sonra salça ilave edip kavurmaya devam edin.
4. Lahanayi, fasulyeyi ve mısırı da içine ilave edip 20 dakika pişirin.
5. Servis etmeden önce baharatları ekleyin.

70 min.

Kale-wasabi-soup (German-Japanese)

Ingredients

- 400 g kale leaves
- 1 onion
- 250 g potatoes
- 100 ml white wine
- 300 ml vegetable broth
- 300 ml sweet cream
- wasabi powder, salt, pepper, sugar, olive oil

30 minutes

Recipe

1. Peel the potatoes and onions and cut them into large pieces. Braise them with olive oil in a pot, quench with white wine, and when the wine has nearly evaporated, add the vegetable broth.
2. When the vegetables are cooked, add the sweet cream and season with salt, sugar, and pepper. Add the finely chopped kale and bring to a boil.
3. Puree everything and pass through a sieve.
4. Season to taste with the wasabi powder.

緑のキャベツとワサビのスープ

Japan

材料

緑のキャベツ　400 g

玉ねぎ　1 個

ジャガイモ　250 g

白ワイン　100 ml

コンソメスープ　300 ml

生クリーム　300 ml

ワサビ、塩、コショウ、砂糖、オリーブオイル

作り方

1．ジャガイモと玉ねぎの皮をむき、一口大に切る。鍋に入れてオリーブオイルでいためる。白ワインをふりかけ、白ワインが煮詰まったらコンソメスープを加える。

2．野菜が柔らかくなったら、生クリームを入れ、塩、砂糖、コショウで味を調える。小さくきざんだ緑のキャベツを加え、一度沸騰させる。

3．2をピューレにし、こし器でこす。

4．好みの量のワサビを入れ、味を調える。

Russian kale soup with zander dumplings

Ingredients

- 1000 g kale
- 1 large onion
- 50 g butter
- $1^1/_2$ l vegetable broth
- 3 Tbsp crème fraiche
- salt
- ground pepper
- ground nutmeg
- 50 g fish filet (zander)
- 40 g sweet cream

Recipe

1. Pluck the kale leaves, cut off the thick stems, select the leaves carefully, wash well, and then blanch in boiling salt water for 3–4 minutes.
2. Drain in a sieve and rinse with cold water.
3. Remove the skin of the onion, chop into fine pieces, and then braise in a pot with butter.
4. Squeeze the water from the kale once again and add to the pot, stir, add the broth and bring to a boil.
5. Simmer the kale in a covered pot for 30–40 minutes, stirring occasionally.
6. Then mix in the crème fraiche, puree the soup, flavor with salt, pepper, and nutmeg, and set aside.
7. Wash and dry the fish filets and then cut them into large pieces, season with salt and pepper, and then puree in a mixer.
8. While pureeing, slowly add the sweet cream, and then drain in a sieve.
9. Bring salt water to a boil and then lower the heat.
10. Form fish dumplings and heat them in the water for 4–5 minutes.
11. Warm up the kale soup, distribute into bowls, place the dumplings on top, and serve immediately.

Russia

Русский суп из зеленой листовой капусты с клецками из судака

Ингредиенты

- 1000 гр. зеленой листовой капусты (кале, грюнколь)
- 1 большая луковица
- 50 г сливочного масла
- 1½ литра овощного бульона
- 3 столовые ложки жирной сметаны
- Соль
- Свежемолотый перец
- Мускатный орех (молотый)
- 50 гр. рыбного филе (судак)
- 40 гр. сливок

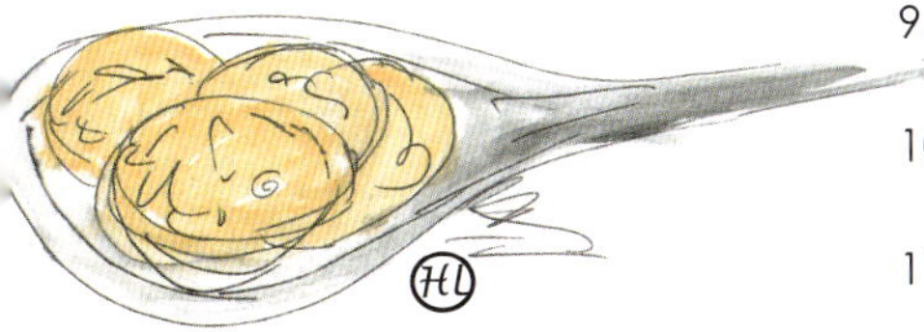

Приготовление

1. Капусту разобрать на листья, перебрать, удалить жесткую часть, тщательно промыть и бланшировать в подсоленной воде в течение 3–4 минут.
2. Слить через сито и обдать холодной водой.
3. Лук очистить, мелко порубить, затем сложить в кастрюлю с растопленным сливочным маслом и притушить.
4. Капусту еще раз отжать и добавить в кастрюлю, перемешать, добавить бульон и довести до кипения.
5. Готовить капусту при закрытой крышке в течение 30–40 мин., периодически помешивая.
6. После того как капуста готова. добавить жирную сметану, добавить соль, перец и мускат, перемешать. Суп взбить погружным блендером до консистенции пюре. Отставить в сторону.
7. Рыбное филе промыть, высушить и порубить, приправить солью и перцем, взбить блендером до консистенции пюре.
8. В процессе взбивания постепенно доба-влять сливки и затем протереть через сито.
9. Вскипятить подсоленную воду и уменьшить температуру.
10. Сформовать рыбные клёцки, опустить в воду и варить 4–5 мин.
11. Подогреть суп из зеленой листовой капусты, разлить по тарелкам, сверху положить рыбные клецки и сразу же подавать к столу.

Salads

Lukewarm kale salad with fried cooked sausage

Ingredients

- 400 g kale leaves
- cooked sausage
- 1 onion
- 1 red onion
- coarse mustard seeds
- mustard
- sugar
- salt
- pepper
- broth
- vinegar

Recipe

1. Cook the sausage in boiling water for 15 minutes.
2. Chop the onion into small pieces and braise in oil. When the onions are glassy, caramelize with a little sugar and quench with vinegar. Cook until only the onions are left. Then add both types of mustard and season with broth, salt, and pepper.
3. Wash the kale, blanch in boiling salt water, and rinse with cold water.
4. Braise strips of red onion in a saucepan, quench with the mustard dressing, add the kale leaves, season again to taste, and serve in the middle of the plates.
5. Cut the cooked sausage in diagonal slices, fry briefly in a pan, then arrange around the kale salad. Serve the salad with a spoonful of dressing.

Lauwarmer Grünkohlsalat mit Kochwurst

Germany

Zutaten

- 400 g Grünkohlblätter
- Kochwürste
- 1 Gemüsezwiebel
- 1 rote Zwiebel
- Grober Senf
- Senf
- Zucker
- Salz
- Pfeffer
- Brühe
- Essig

Zubereitung

1. Die Kochwurst in heißem Wasser für 15 Minuten köcheln lassen.
2. Die Gemüsezwiebel in feine Würfel schneiden und in etwas Öl anschwitzen. Wenn die Zwiebelwürfel glasig sind mit ein wenig Zucker karamellisieren und mit Essig ablöschen. Diesen dann so weit einkochen, bis nur noch die Zwiebeln übrig sind. Danach die beiden Senfsorten dazugeben und mit Brühe, Salz und Pfeffer abschmecken.
3. Den Grünkohl waschen, in Salzwasser blanchieren, und in kaltem Wasser abschrecken.
4. In einer Pfanne die in Streifen geschnittene rote Zwiebel anschwitzen, mit dem Senfdressing ablöschen und die Grünkohlblätter hinzugeben, nochmals abschmecken und in die Mitte eines Tellers anrichten.
5. Die Kochwurst schräg in Scheiben schneiden, in einer Pfanne kurz anbraten und dann um den Grünkohlsalat legen. Mit einem Löffel ein wenig Dressing um den Salat anrichten.

Danish kale salad with nuts and apples

Ingredients

- 300 g kale
- 200 g apples (Boskop)
- 100 g hazelnuts
- 40 g raisins

Dressing
- 1 Tbsp apple vinegar
- 1 cup freshly pressed orange juice
- 1/2 Tbsp liquid honey
- 1 1/2 cups sweet cream

30 minutes

Recipe

1. Warm the nuts briefly in a pan without oil to enhance the taste.
2. Cut kale leaves from the stems, wash thoroughly, dry, and mix together with the nuts in a kitchen mixer.
3. Cut the apples into very small pieces and mix into the salad.
4. Prepare the dressing (without the cream) and mix into the salad.
5. Whip the cream and mix it into the salad as well.
6. It will all taste delicious!

Grønkålsalader

Denmark

Ingredienser

- 300 g Grønkål/palmekål
- 200 g madæbler
- 100 g hasselnødder
- 40 g rosiner

Dressing:
- 1 spsk Æbleeddike
- 1 dl friskpresset appelsinsaft
- 1/2 spsk flydende honing
- 1 1/2 dl Piskefløde/sojafløde

Sådan gør du:

1. Rist nødderne på en tør pande for at fremhæve smagen.
2. Grønkålsbladene skæres fra stokken, skylles grundigt, afdryppes og blendes i en foodprocessor sammen med hasselnødderne.
3. Æblerne skæres i bittesmå terninger og blandes i salaten.
4. Dressingen røres sammen (Minus fløden) og blandes i grønkålen.
5. Fløden piskes og vendes i til sidst i salaten.

30 Min.

Salad with kale and red currants

Ingredients

- 750 g kale
- 350 g red currants (frozen) or 4 Tbsp red currant jelly
- 6 cloves of garlic
- 4 Tbsp salad oil
- salt, pepper, and sugar to season
- 3 hard-boiled eggs

40 minutes

Recipe

1. Mix 200 g red currants and drain in a sieve. Mix with oil, pressed garlic cloves, salt, pepper, and sugar.
2. Blanch the kale (freed of the hard stems) briefly in boiling water and drain. Rinse with cold water, dry on paper towels, cut into thin strips and place on a dish.
3. Mix the fruit sauce together with the remaining red currants, distribute over the kale, and garnish with the chopped eggs.

Sałatka z jarmużu z porzeczkami

Poland

składniki

- 750 g liści jarmużu
- 350 g czerwonych porzeczek (mrożonych) lub
- 4 łyżki galaretki porzeczkowej
- 6 ząbków czosnku
- 4 łyżki oleju sałatkowego
- Sól, pieprz, Cukier do smaku
- 3 jajka ugotowane na twardo

przygotowanie

1. Porzeczki (200 g) miksujemy, przecieramy przez sito, mieszamy z olejem roztartym z solą, czosnkiem, pieprzem i cukrem, lekko schładzamy.
2. Pozbawione twardych ogonków liście jarmużu wrzucamy na 2 minuty na lekko osolony wrzątek, odcedzamy, przelewamy zimną wodą, osuszamy, kroimy w cieńkie paski.
3. Polewamy sosem, łączymy z pozostałymi porzeczkami, mieszamy, posypujemy posiekanymi jajkami.

Stews

Stewed kale – the modern version

Ingredients

- 1 kg fresh, washed kale
- 300 ml sweet heavy cream (38%)
- 1 lemon (juice)
- 50 g coarse mustard seeds

30 Minuten

Recipe

1. Remove the tough middle stems from the kale and rinse the rest in cold water. Place the kale in a casserole dish with cold water and bring to a boil.
2. Cook further for about 3 minutes without a cover, stirring occasionally. Then leave the kale to cool, drain the water, and chop the kale into large pieces.
3. Heat up the cream until it begins to thicken; season with salt, lemon juice, and mustard. Mix the kale together with the cream and serve hot.

Stuvet grønkål – moderne

Denmark

Ingredienser

- 1 kg grønkål – urenset vægt
- 3 dl piskefløde Havsalt
- 1 citron – saften heraf
- 50 g grov sennep

30 minutter

Sådan gør du

Fjern de groveste midter-ribber på grønkålen, og rens resten for jord i koldt vand. Sæt grønkålen over i koldt vand, og lad den få ca. 3 minutter i kogende vand – uden låg! Og husk at vende den løbende. Tag den op af vandet, lad den køle af, vrid den fri for vand, og skær den i grove stykker. Kog piskefløden ind til en let cremet konsistens, smag til med salt, citronsaft og grov sennep. Vend kålen i denne fløde-creme, og varm det hele hurtigt op, før servering.

Mash pot – hearty Dutch specialty

Ingredients

- 1 kg kale
- 300 ml water
- 1 kg mealy potatoes
- 70 g lard
- 750 g smoked sausage
- 3 onions
- 200 g bacon
- 1 broth cube
- 3 Tbsp white wine vinegar
- freshly ground black or white pepper
- salt from the mill

60 minutes

A tip from the kale-gourmet-team: Can be served with gravy.

Recipe

1. Peel the potatoes, cut into quarters, and keep in water until used. Wash kale, remove leaves, and chop finely. Dice the bacon, cut the onions into rings. Place potatoes in a large pot and fill up with water. Add a broth cube. Place the kale over the potatoes, overlay with the smoked sausage. Bring to a boil in the covered pot. Then simmer at low heat for 20–25 minutes.
2. Add the bacon pieces to a small frying pan and braise until glassy, then add the onions. Simmer at low heat for 15 minutes. If you prefer the bacon to be browner, remove the cover and raise the heat.
3. When the potatoes are cooked, remove the smoked sausage. Transfer the potatoes and kale to a bowl. Mash the potatoes and kale coarsely, but not too smooth. A mash pot is not mashed potatoes! Add some of the cooking broth to ensure that the vegetable mass remains soft.
4. Fold in the onions and bacon pieces. Add pepper, lard, and vinegar. If salt should be added depends on the taste of the cook. Each person can add his/her own salt from the mill on the table.
5. The mash pot should be served piping hot. Garnish with pieces or slices of the smoked sausage.

Stevige Nederlandse boerenkoolstamppot

Netherlands

Ingrediënten

- 1 kg boerenkool
- 0,3 l water
- 1 kg kruimige aardappels
- 70 g reuzel of vet
- 750 g rookworst
- 3 uien
- 200 g ontbijtspek
- 1 bouillonblokje
- 3 eetlepels wittewijn-azijn
- vers gemalen zwarte of witte peper
- zout uit het molentje.

60 minuten

De speciale tip van het boerenkool gourmet team: Er kan braadjus bij geserveerd worden.

Bereiding

1. De aardappels schillen, in vieren delen en tot aan het gebruik in water leggen. Boerenkoolstronken wassen, plukken en klein snijden. Het spek in dobbelsteentjes en de uien in ringen snijden. De aardappels in een grote pan doen, met water opvullen. Een bouillonblokje erbij doen. De boerenkool op de aardappels leggen en daarbovenop de rookworst. Met gesloten deksel aan de kook brengen. En dan 20–25 minuten op klein vuur zachtjes laten doorkoken.
2. De spekdobbelsteentjes in een kleine pan doen en het spek glazig smoren. Als het spek uitgebakken is de uien erbij doen. En nog 15 minuten op klein vuur laten trekken. Als je het spek wat bruiner wil hebben, kun je aan het einde de deksel eraf halen en het vuur hoger draaien.
3. Als de aardappels helemaal gaar zijn die rookworst eraf halen. De aardappels met de boerenkool in een schotel afgieten Met een stamper de aardappelen boerenkool grof fijnstampen. Het moet niet te fijn zijn, het is geen puree! Kookvocht erbij doen, zodat een soepele massa ontstaat.
4. Uien en spekdobbelsteentjes erdoor roeren. Peper, reuzel en de azijn erbij doen. Of er nog zout aan toegevoegd wordt hangt van de smaak van de kok af. Met een zoutstrooier op tafel kan ieder zijn eigen portie op smaak brengen.
5. De stamppot wordt nog dampend in de pan geserveerd. De rookworst wordt in stukken of plakjes gesneden daarboven op gegarneerd.

Hearty Hungarian kale stew

Ingredients

- 1.5 kg kale
- salt
- pepper from the mill
- 600 g potatoes
- 400 g carrots
- 3 onions
- 3 Tbsp oil
- 1.5 l vegetable broth
- 6 cooked sausages

60 minutes

A tip from our kale-gourmet-team: A pinch of paprika rounds out the flavor.

Recipe

1 Kale: clean, rinse, and blanch for about 3 minutes in boiling salted water. Remove the kale, drain, let cool. Chop into small pieces.

2. Peel the potatoes and carrots. Chop the onions into small dices.
3. Heat the oil in a pot. Braise the onions, add the kale. Cook for 5 minutes, add the broth, bring to a boil, and simmer with the cover on for about 20 minutes.
4. Cut the potatoes and carrots into small squares, add to the pot and blend in.
5. Lay the sausages on top and cook covered for a further 15 minutes.
6. Season the kale with salt and pepper. Serve the stew in a terrine with a small side dish of mustard.

Bőséges marhakáposztatál magyarosan

Hungary

Hozzávalók

- 1,5 kg marhakáposzta
- só
- törött bors
- 600 g (60 dkg) krumpli
- 400 g (40 dkg) sárgarépa
- 3 vöröshagyma
- 3 evőkanál olaj
- 1,5 l zöldséglé
- 6 főzőkolbász (debreceni) vagy virsli

Főzési idő: 60 perc

A marhakáposzta-gourmet-csoport különleges tanácsa: Egy csipetnyi pirospaprika teljessé teszi, kikerekíti az étel ízét.

Elkészítés:

1. A marhakáposztát megpucoljuk, megmossuk és forrásban lévő sósvízben kb. 3 percig főzzük. A marhakáposztát kivesszük a vízből, lecsöpögtetjük és lehűtjük, majd apró darabokra vágjuk.
2. A krumplit és a sárgarépát megpucoljuk. A hagymát apróra vágjuk.
3. Az olajat egy lábasban felforrósítjuk és a hagymát megdínszteljük, majd hozzáadjuk a káposztát. Körülbelül 5 percig dínszteljük, hozzáadjuk a zöldséglevet, felforraljuk és fedő alatt kb. 20 percig kis lángon főzzük.
4. A krumplit és a répát hozzákeverjük.
5. A főzőkolbászt rárakjuk és csukott fedő alatt további 15 percig kis lángon főzzük.
6. A marhakáposztát sóval és borssal szervírozzuk. A főzeléket egy nagy tálban szervírozzuk és egy kis tálban mustárt kínálunk hozzá.

Kale from Libya

Ingredients

- 100 g red lentils
- 750 g kale
- 200 g onions
- 3 cloves of garlic
- 1 1/2 red pepper
- 1 1/2 yellow pepper
- 2 Tbsp of curry (or more, if desired)
- 1/2 tsp green cardamom
- 100 ml vegetable broth (or more, if desired)
- 300 g feta cheese
- 60 g roasted pine nuts
- 1/2 tsp salt
- pepper
- brown rice

Recipe

1. Soak lentils in cold water for 30 minutes. Cut the stems off the kale leaves, wash leaves thoroughly. Blanch for 2 minutes in a large pot of boiling salted water, decant, rinse with cold water, drain.
2. Chop the onions and garlic cloves into small pieces, the peppers into cubes. Braise the onions and garlic in hot olive oil, add curry and cardamom, simmer together. Add the peppers and cook for 2 more minutes.
3. Add the kale and drained lentils, fill up with broth and cook for 3–5 minutes. Season to taste. Finally, cut the cheese into small cubes, blend in, and sprinkle the roasted pine nuts over the stew.
4. Serve with basmati or brown rice.

معاشرة الادن

Libya

وصفة رقم ١٢

ملفوف اخضر

المستلزمات

- ٠٠ غرام عدس احمر
- ٧٥٠ غرام ملفوف اخضر
- ٢٠٠ غرام بصل
- ٢ حبات ثوم (رسو ثوم)
- ٠٫٥ فلفلة حمراء
- ٠٫٥ فلفلة صفراء
- ملعقتان طماطم كمون ويمكن زيادة
- ½ ملعقة شاي حب الآل اخضر
- ١٠٠ غرام مرقة خضار ويمكن زيادة
- ٢٠٠ غرام جبنة غنم
- ٦٠ غرام صنوبر مقلي
- ملح
- ½ ملعقة شاي ؟
- ... غير مقشور (طبيعي)

التحضير.

١- ينقع العدس ولمدة ٢ دقيقة في الماء البارد حتى يلين يستبعد من ورق الملفوف العروق ومن منتصف الورقة ويغسل جيداً ويوضع ولمدة دقيقتان في الماء المغلي والمملح بعد ذلك يغسل بماء بارد ويجفف

٢- يفرم البصل والثوم + تفرم الفلفلة منفردة ويوضع البصل والثوم المفروم في زيت القلي ذو الحرارة المعتدلة وكذلك يضاف الى الكمون وحب الآل ويحرك ذلك لمدة قصيرة حتى يصبح اللون ذهبياً مع الفلفل ويترك ذلك لمدة دقيقتان حتى ينضج

٣- يضاف الى الخليط الملفوف الذي تكون قد جف وكذلك العدس ويضاف اليه الملح ومرقة الخضار ويترك ذلك لمدة ٢-٥ دقائق حتى ينضج ويرش على ذلك البهارات وفي النهاية تقطع الجبنة على شكل مكعبات وتوضع في الخلط ومن ثم يرش الصنوبر المقلي على ذلك

٤- يؤكل الى جانب ذلك رز باسماتي غير مقشور او رز طبيعي

وصفة خاصة ذاتي الملفوف الاخضر.

The Ethiopian classic – kale stew

Ingredients

- 1 kg kale
- 3 large potatoes
- 2 stalks of leeks
- 2 pepperoni
- 3/4 cup olive oil
- 2 small onions
- 5 cloves of garlic
- 1/2 tsp ground ginger
- salt

40 minutes

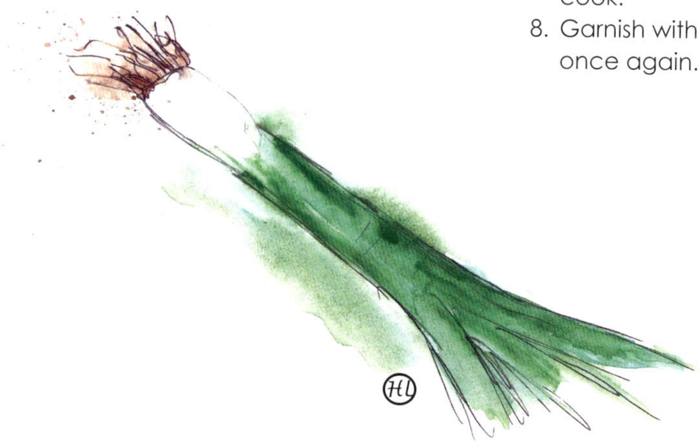

Recipe

1. Kale: Remove leaves and cook in salted water.
2. Peel the potatoes and cut into small cubes.
3. Wash the white part of the leek stalks and chop into small cubes.
4. Halve the pepperoni, remove the seeds, and cut into long strips. Save 1/3 of the strips for garnishing.
5. Heat oil in a pot, braise the onions until brown. Add the leeks and fry quickly.
6. Pour in a cup of water and then add the kale. At a medium temperature cook for 20 minutes.
7. Blend in the potatoes, pressed garlic, ginger and a pinch of salt and continue to cook.
8. Garnish with pepperoni and cook briefly once again.

ቅቅል የሃበሻ ገመን

Ethiopia

ግብአቶች

- 1000 ግራም የሃበሻ ጎመን
- 3 ትልልቅ ድንች
- 2 እግር ባሮ
- 2 ቃሪያ
- ሦስት አራተኛ ስኒ የወይራ ዘይት
- 2 ትንንሽ የተከተፈ ቀይ ሽንኩርት
- 5 ፍንካች ነጭ ሽንኩርት
- ግማሽ የሻይ ማንኪያ የተፈጨ ዝንጅብል
- ጨው

40 ደቂቃ

አሠራር.

1. የአበሻ ጎመን: የጎመኑን ቅጥል በረጅሙና በቁመቱ መቁረጥና ውሃ ውስጥ ትንሽ ጨው ጨምሮ መቀቀል።
2. ድንቹን መላጥና በትንንሹ መቁረጥ።
3. የባሮውን ነጭ አካል ማጠብና በትንንሹ መቁረጥ።
4. ቃሪያውን ሰንጥቆ ፍሬውን ማውጣትና በረጅሙ መክተፍ፣ ሲሶውን ለማጌጫ ወይም ማሳመሪያ ማስቀመጥ።
5. ድስት ወይም ብረት ድስት ውስጥ ዘይቱ ቡናማ ቀለም እስኪሆነው ድረስ ማሞቅ፣ ባሮውን ጨምሮ ለአጭር ጊዜ ማብሰል።
6. አንድ ስኒ ውሃ መጨመርና ከጎመኑ ጋር በመሃከለኛ ሙቀት 20 ደቂቃ መቀቀል።
7. ድንቹን ከነጭ ሽንኩርት ጭማቂ፣ ዝንጅብልና ትንሽ ጨው ጋር ማማሰልና ማብሰል።
8. ለጣእሙ ቃሪያ ማላስና ለአጭር ጊዜ መቀቀል።

Christmas kale

The journey of our local consultant Dr. Sigvor Bakke to kale

Kale grew for many years hidden in our huge garden in Vågseidet near a fjord close to Bergen. Between all the berries, bushes, flowers and trees, it remained invisible to our family. For several decades of my life, I never saw it, neither in Norway nor in the USA, Spain, or Peru, in which countries I lived for several years. It was not until my later husband informed me in Lima that I would get to know kale with Pinkel sausage in Bremen. It would be an exaggeration to claim that that was the reason I came to Bremen, but once I was there, I came to love kale. Not only that: my husband brought all the necessary ingredients to Bergen where we first enjoyed at Christmas a feast of ham, hearty German sausages, and Bremer and Oldenburger Pinkel sausages with the kale long ignored from our own garden. My parents were so excited that they started to search for Norwegian kale recipes. And we were successful! In the attic we found in a book of my grandparents from 1930: a kale recipe! Did they plant the kale? From now on, in our increasingly globalized world, we use international kale variations of our family recipe – in my family's home together with the lovingly cultivated kale from our own wonderful garden!

Min lange reisen til den norske grønnkålen

Grønnkål vokste i mange å i vår store hage på Vågseidet som ligger ved fjord i nærheten av Bergen i Norge. Mellom alle blomster, bærbusker og trær ble den så og si uoppdaget av vår familie. Gjennom mange tiår hadde jeg aldri spist denne grønnsaken, hverken i Norge, USA, Spania eller i Peru der jeg bodde i mange år. Det var først i Lima at min senere ektemann fortalte meg at jeg nok kom til å bli kjent med »Grünkohl und Pinkel« i Bremen. Det ville være en overdrivelse å hevde jeg kom til Bremen av den grunn, men da jeg først var kommet hit lærte også å sette pris på grønnkålen. Men ikke bare det, min mann tok alle nødvendige ingrediensene med til Norge, og nå spiste vi for første gang i julehelgen »Kassler«, tyske kraftige pølser, Bremer og Oldenburger Pinkel sammen grønnkål fra vår egen hage – som ingen riktig hadde brydd seg om tidligere. Mine foreldre var så begeistret for denne retten at vi begynte å lete etter norske grønnkål-oppskrifter – og på loftet fant vi en kokebok fra 1930! som hadde tilhørt min besteforeldre – og der var det sannelig en grønnkål-oppskrift! Hadde kanskje de plantet grønnkålen en gang i tiden? Fremdeles finnes det – i en stadig mer globalisert verden – også noen internasjonale grønnkålvariasjoner på vår private spiseplan, og familien min i Norge har nå den velpleide grønnkålen direkte fra vår vakre hage!

Stuet grønnkål

Norway

Ingredients

- 250 g kale
- 30 g (2 Tbsp) butter
- 30 g (2 Tbsp) flour
- 400–500 ml milk
- sugar
- a pinch of salt
- a pinch of pepper, freshly ground
- a pinch of nutmeg
- lemon juice (if desired)

Recipe

1. Kale: Remove the thick stems and veins, chop into fine pieces, wash thoroughly, and drain to dry.
2. Simmer the kale in salted water for 15–20 minutes.
3. Prepare the Bechamel sauce.
4. Add the kale and simmer for a further 10–15 minutes at medium heat.
5. Season to taste with salt, nutmeg, and pepper (and lemon juice, if desired).

25 minutes

A tip from our kale-gourmet-team: In Norway »stuing« is often used and it goes well with meat or fish. Instead of kale, which is often not available, white cabbage, turnips, or peas can be used. The dish is especially tasty when one prepares the Bechamel sauce with some of the broth. A little sweet cream tops off the taste.

Ingredienser

- 250 g renset grønnkål
- 30 g smør
- 30 g hvetemel
- 4–5 dl melk
- 1 ts salt
- 1 ts pepper
- 1 ts muskat
- evtl. litt sitronsaft

Tilberedning

1. Vask, rens, hakk og forvell grønnkålen I lettsaltet vann
2. Lag hvit saus
3. Ha kålen i, og la den koke i sausen i 10–15 minutter
4. Smak til med salt, pepper og muskatt (evtl. litt sitronsaft)

Bigos kale

Ingredients

- 1.5 kg kale
- 1 large apple
- 3 onions
- 450 g boiled sausage
- 1 tsp caraway
- 1 Tbsp lard
- 1 Tbsp butter
- 1 Tbsp flour
- salt, pepper, and sugar
- 1 Tbsp lemon juice
- 1 glass vegetable broth

40 minutes

Recipe

1. Remove kale leaves from the thick stems. Blanch the leaves, drain through a sieve, rinse with cold water, and cut into thin strips.
2. Place the kale in a pot and simmer uncovered with vegetable broth, caraway, salt, pepper, and sugar.
3. Melt the lard in a frying pan, braise the finely diced onions and sausage cut into slices, and add to the kale.
4. Add the peeled and sliced apple.
5. Thicken with flour and butter, if desired.
6. Season to taste with lemon juice, salt and pepper.
7. Serve the kale bigos (Polish stew) on the side or with potatoes.

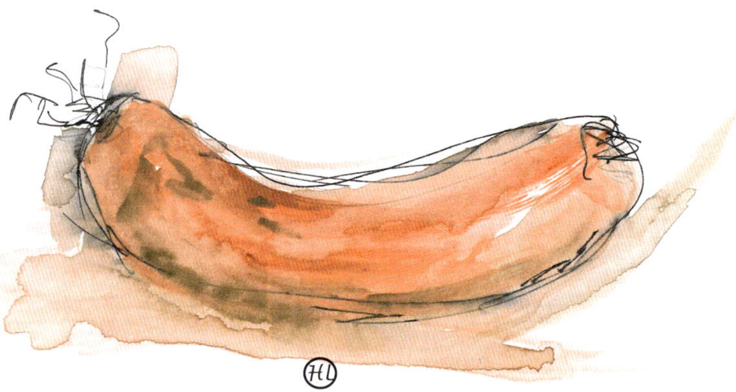

Bigosik z jarmużu

Poland

składniki

- 1,5 kg jarmużu
- duże winne jabłko
- 3 cebule
- 450 g kiełbasy wieprzowej
- Łyżeczka kminku
- Łyżka smalcu
- Łyżka masła
- Łyżka mąki
- śol, pieprz
- cukier
- łyżka soku z cyrtryny
- szklanka bullionu

przygotowanie

1. Z liści wycinamy grube nerwy. Liście wrzucamy na wrzątek i gotujemy kilka minut. Wyjmujemy. Przelewamy zimną wodą. Osączamy, kroimy w cienkie paski. Wkładamy do rondla, zalewamy gorącym bulionem, wrzucamy kminek, śol, pieprz, cukier i gotujemy na niewielkim ogniu bez przykrycia. Na palenti rozgrzewamy smalec, przesmażamy na nim pokrojoną cebulę, dodajemy pokrojoną w plasterski kiełbasę i chwilę smażymy. Dodajemy do jarmużu razem z obranym ogniu. Zagęzcamy zasmażką z masła i mąki. Doprawiamy do smaku sokiem z cytryny, pieprzem i solą.
2. Podajemy jako gorącą przystawkę lub z ziemniakami z wody.

Kale with ham and eggs

Ingredients

- 2 kg fresh kale (ready for cooking)
- 150 g diced ham
- 150 g diced onions
- 0.4 l hot vegetable broth
- salt, freshly ground black pepper (for seasoning to taste)
- 1½ pinches of freshly ground nutmeg
- 2 peeled raw potatoes
- 12 thin slices of bacon
- 6 eggs

90 minutes

Recipe

1. Kale: wash, drain, and remove the leaves.
2. Braise the diced ham in a pot, add the diced onions and continue to braise.
3. Add the kale and cook for a few minutes while stirring.
4. Heat up the vegetable broth, pour into the kale pot and season with salt, pepper, and nutmeg. Simmer at low heat for about 60 minutes.
5. Grate the potatoes into the kale and simmer for 5 more minutes. Place the kale in a prewarmed casserole dish and keep warm.
6. Fry the bacon strips in a frying pan (without oil) until crispy. Crack the eggs, slide them onto the bacon strips, add salt, and cook over low heat for about 6 minutes.
7. Decorate the kale with the eggs and bacon and serve.
8. Fried potatoes make a perfect side dish.

jarmuż z boczkiem i jajami

Poland

składniki

- 2 kg jarmużu
- 150 g pokrojonego w kostkę boczku
- 150 g cebuli, pokrojonej w kostkę
- 0,4 l gorącego rosołu z mięsa
- Sól i świeżo zmielony czarny pieprz (do smaku)
- Świeżo startej gałki muszkatowej (do smaku)
- 2 obrane surowe ziemniaki
- 12 cienkich plastrów boczku
- 6 jajka

90 minut

przygotowanie

1. Jarmuż umyć i osaczyć
2. Boczek na patelni podsmarzyć, dodać cebulę i dalej smarzyc.
3. Jarmuzu dodac i mieszajac gotować kilka minut.
4. Wlać cieply bulion i doprawić solą, pieprzem i gałką muszkatową. Gotować na wolnym ogniu przez 60 minut.
5. Ocierane ziemniaki dodac do jarmużu i gotować kolejne 5 minut. Jarmuż dać w podgrzana miske.
6. Plasterki boczku na patelni ostro podsmarzyć. Jajka rozbic i rozpuścić na boczku, około 6 minut dalej smarzyć.
7. Boczek z jajami na jarmuż polozyc.
8. Smażone ziemniaki podac jako przystawkę.

Lasagne with kale and mushrooms

Ingredients

- 20 g dried mushrooms or 300 g fresh mushrooms
- 400 g kale
- 200 g sweet cream
- 1 large onion
- salt, pepper, thyme
- 2 Tbsp olive oil
- 100 g emmental or pecorino cheese
- 1 Tbsp flour
- 300 g pureed tomato
- 8 lasagne sheets
- 1 bunch of parsley

Recipe

1. Pour boiling water over the mushrooms and allow to soak for 1 hour. Drain the mushrooms and collect the water for quenching the onions later.
2. Wash the kale and cut into strips. Cut the onions into small dices and chop the parsley into small pieces.
3. Braise the onions in hot oil and add the chopped mushrooms. Sprinkle with flour and quench with the rinse water above. Add the kale and simmer for 15 minutes.
4. Blend in the tomatoes, parsley, and cream and season to taste with salt, pepper, and thyme. Grate the cheese.
5. In a prewarmed casserole dish, add one after the other sheets of lasagne, kale sauce, and grated cheese, ending with the kale sauce and cheese on top.
6. Place the casserole in the middle of oven preheated to 220 °C (gas: level 4) and bake for about 30–45 minutes, until the lasagne is soft.

Lasagne con cavolo verde e funghi

Italy

Ingredienti

- 20 g di funghi porcini secchi o ca. 300 g di funghi freschi
- 400 g di cavolo verde
- 200 g di panna
- 1 cipolla (grande)
- sale, pepe, timo
- 2 cucchiai di olio d`oliva
- 100 g di pecorino o groviera
- 1 cucchiaio di farina
- 300 g di passato di pomodoro
- 8 fogli di lasagne
- 1 mazzetto di prezzemolo

Preparazione:

1. Bagnare i funghi porcini in acqua bollente, e far ammollare per 1 ora. Sgocciolarli e mettere da parte il sugo.
2. Pulire il cavolo verde e tagliare a striscie. Tritare la cipolla e il prezzemolo.
3. Soffriggere la cipolla tritata nell'olio, poi versare i funghi. Aggiungere un po' di farina e l'acqua dei funghi. Poi aggiungere il cavolo verde e far cuocere per circa 15 minuti.
4. Aggiungere il passato di pomodoro, il prezzemolo, la panna e aggiustare di sale, pepe e timo. Grattugiare il formaggio.
5. Riscaldare una pirofila. Mettervi a strati i fogli di lasagne, ricoprendo ogni strato con una parte del sugo e una spruzzata di formaggio grattugiato. Lultimo strato sarà di formaggio col resto di sugo.
6. Mettere nel forno ben caldo a 220° per 30–45 minuti (forno a gas grado 4), finché la pasta sarà cotta.

Turkish kale/barley casserole with lamb meatballs

Ingredients

- 3/4 cup barley
- 1 kg ground lamb
- 2 onions, chopped
- 5 Tbsp finely chopped parsley
- 3/4 cup fresh breadcrumbs
- 2 egg yolks
- 2 cups chicken broth
- 1 pinch of ground allspice
- 1/4 tsp freshly grated nutmeg
- 1 tsp salt
- 1/2 tsp freshly ground pepper
- 1 kg kale (or 1/2 kg without the stems)
- 1 Tbsp olive oil
- 1.5 Tbsp butter
- 3 pressed cloves of garlic
- 2 tsp ground coriander
- 1.5 containers of sour cream

70 minutes

A tip from our kale-gourmet-team: Add a pinch of allspice to the kale mixture, as well.

Recipe

1. Kale: Remove the leaves, wash, and cut into large pieces.
2. Cook the barley in a large pot with boiling salt water for about 20 minutes.
3. Mix together in a separate pot: Ground lamb, onions, breadcrumbs, egg yolks, ½ cup chicken broth, allspice, nutmeg, ½ tsp salt, and pepper. Form small meatballs.
4. Heat oil in a frying pan and fry the meatballs until crispy. Place aside.
5. Warm up the butter in a pot, add the kale and ½ cup chicken broth, and cook for about 20 minutes.
6. Mix together the garlic, remaining salt, and coriander until it forms a paste-like mass. Heat up a tsp of olive oil in a small frying pan at low heat and braise the garlic mass for about 3 minutes until it is golden brown.
7. Blend the garlic mass in the kale. Then mix in the barley and the last ½ cup of chicken broth as well as (carefully!) the meatballs. Simmer at low heat for 30 minutes.
8. Just before serving blend in the sour cream. Keep the pot on the stove for a moment.

Türk usulü Karalahana/Arpalı Köfte Suflesi

Turkey

Malzemeler

- ¾ fincan arpa
- 1 kilo kuzu kıyması
- 2 doğranmış soğan
- 5 yemek kaşıgı ince kıyılmıs maydanoz
- ¾ fincan ufalanmış ekmek
- 2 yumurta sarısı
- 2 fincan tavuk suyu
- Bir tutam çekilmiş yenibahar
- ¼ taze rendelenmiş hindistan cevizi
- 1 çay kaşığı tuz
- ½ taze öğütülmüs karabiber
- 1 kilo kara lahana (veya sapsız ise yarım kilo)
- 1 yemek kaşığı zeytinyagı
- 1,5 yemek kaşığı tereyağı
- 3 dis ezilmiş sarımsak
- 2 çay kaşığı çekilmiş kişniş
- 1,5 bardak ekşi krema

Pişme Süresi: 70 dakika

Karalahana gurme-ekibinin tavsiyesi: Karalahananin icine yenibahar koyun.

Hazırlanışı

1. Kara lahananın yapraklarını koparın, yıkayın ve iri iri kesin.
2. Arpayı büyük bir tencerenin icinde tuzunu ilave edip suda aşağı yukarı 20 dakika pişirin.
3. Kıymayı, soğanı, ufalanmıs ekmeği, yumurta sarısını, tavuk suyunun yarısını, yenibaharı, hindistan cevizini, yarım çaykasığı tuzu ve karabiberi bir kapta karıştırarak yoğurun. hemen arkasından top, top köfte haline getirin.
4. Başka bir tencerede tere yağını eritip ve hazırlanmış lahanayı ve kalan tavuk suyunu ilave edip yaklaşik 20 dakika pişirin.
5. Tereyağı bir tencerede ısıtın. hazırlanmıs yeşil lahanayı ve diğer yarım fincan tavuk suyunuda tencereye ilave edin ve aşağı yukarı 20 dakika pişirin.
6. Sarımsağı, kalan tuzu ve kimyonu ezme kıvamına gelene kadar karıştırın. küçük tavada bir çaykasığı zeytinyagını orta ateşte kızdırın ve ezilmiş, sarımsak karışımını 3 dakika sararana kadar kızartın.
7. Sarımsak karışımını lahanaya ilave edip karıştırın. sonradan kalan yarım fıncan tavuk suyunu ve top top köftelerini içine koyun.
8. Servis yapmadan önce ekşi kremayı icine karıştırın. Ocağın altını kapatıp yemegi biraz daha bekletin.

Pesto and Marmalade

Kale marmalade

Ingredients

- 300 g fresh kale leaves
- 100 g jam sugar 1:3
- 1 vanilla pod

30 minutes

Tip from our kale-gourmet-team: Kale marmalade goes especially well with a cheese platter.

Recipe

1. Kale: Wash well, drain, remove the leaves, and cut leaves into small pieces.
2. Cook the chopped kale together with the gelling sugar and contents of the vanilla pod.
3. Pour the marmalade into marmalade jars rinsed with hot water, seal, and allow to cool.

Grünkohlmarmelade

Germany

Zutaten

- 300 g Grünkohlblätter, frisch
- 100 g Gelierzucker 1:3
- 1 St. Vanilleschote

30 Minuten

Der besondere Tipp des Grünkohl-Gourmetteams: Die Grünkohlmarmelade passt sehr gut zu einer kleinen Käseplatte.

Vorbereitung

1. Den Grünkohl gut waschen, abtropfen und Blätter abstreifen, in kleine Stücke schneiden.
2. Den zerkleinerten Grünkohl mit dem Gelierzucker und dem Mark von der Vanilleschote aufkochen.
3. Die Marmelade in ein heiß ausgespültes Glas füllen, fest verschließen und abkühlen lassen.

Spaghetti with kale pesto and pecorino cheese

Ingredients

- 400 g spaghetti
- 10 leaves of kale
- 2 small cloves of garlic
- 150 ml olive oil
- juice from half a lemon
- 75 g pine nuts
- salt
- 150 g apricots
- 150 g dried tomatoes
- 100 g pecorino cheese

Recipe

1. Remove the leaves of kale from the stems, wash, and drain.
2. Puree in a small container – together with the oil – the finely chopped apricots and tomatoes, lemon juice, salt, and garlic. Then add the pine nuts and puree briefly to chop the nuts.
3. Cook the spaghetti for 6 minutes in water with a tsp of salt, drain, and allow to cool in a heated pot.
4. Fold the pesto into the spaghetti, sprinkle with pecorino cheese, and serve.
5. Alternative: Serve the cheese separately so that each guest can add as desired.

Spaghetti con pesto di cavolo verde e pecorino

Italy

Ingredienti

- 400 g di spaghetti
- 10 foglie die cavolo verde
- 2 spicchi d'aglio
- 150 ml d'olio d'oliva
- succo di mezzo limone
- 75 g di pinoli
- sale
- 150 g di albicocca
- 150 g pomodori secchi
- 100 g di pecorino

Preparazione

1. Pulire il cavolo verde, separare il verde dal gambo, lavare e asciugare.
2. In un frullatore mettere l'olio, le albicocche macinate e i pomodori, il succo di limone, sale e l'aglio. Finalmente aggiungere i pinoli.
3. Scolare gli spaghetti al dente.
4. Conditeli con il pesto e il pecorino.
5. Alternativa: Servire separate, così ognuno si prepara il suo piatto a piacere.

Old English mushroom pudding on curly kale

Great Britain

Ingredients

Filling
- 600 g beef; roughly diced
- 400 g mushrooms; mixed
- 2 onions, diced
- 4 Tbsp flour
- 200 ml beef broth (granulated broth)
- Worcestershire sauce
- celery salt
- pepper

Dough
- 300 g flour
- 1 tsp salt
- 8 Tbsp butter
- 200 ml water, ice cold

Curly Kale as Side Dish
- 500 g curly kale
- 1 onion
- salt, pepper

2.5 hours

Recipe

1. To make the pastry, sift the flour and salt into a bowl and stir in flakes of butter. Add all the water and stir with a knife to form loose dough. Turn out onto a floured surface and knead shortly. Brush a 1.2 l pudding mould with oil or butter. Roll out the dough with a dusting of flour to form a circle of 25 cm in diameter. Cut out a quarter section and save for top, line the pudding mould and set aside.
2. Mix beef, mushrooms, onions, flour and seasoning in a bowl, transfer to the pastry-lined pudding mould. Add some dashes of Worcestershire sauce and beef broth.
3. Bring overlapping pastry edges towards the center, moisten with water and cover the top with the leftover pastry. Place a circle of baking parchment on top of the pastry, then cover the whole pudding mould with tin foil.
4. Fill 5 cm water in a sauce pan and bring it to boil. After water boils, lower the pudding mould into the pan and cover with the lid. Steam for 2½ hours, making sure the water doesn't boil out – add more if needed.
5. When ready to serve, turn the pudding out of the mould onto a serving plate.
6. Serve with curly kale as side dish. (Curly kale should be cooked for 60 minutes along with onions, salt, and pepper.)

Quiche, Cakes, and Pizza

Kale quiche

Ingredients

- 375 g flour
- 200 g soft butter
- 3 Tbsp water
- 1 1/2 pinches of salt
- 400 g kale
- 3 scallions
- black pepper
- 230 g grated cheese (cheddar)
- 180 g chopped walnuts
- 4 1/2 eggs
- 1 clove of garlic
- 2 thyme sprigs
- 300 ml sweet cream
- 150 ml milk

Recipe

1. Prepare pastry from the flour, butter, water, and salt and layer into a greased 24 cm quiche form.
2. Bake the pastry for 10 minutes in a preheated 200°C oven.
3. Chop the scallions and mix under the cooked kale. Season to taste with salt and pepper. Blend in the grated cheddar cheese and the chopped walnuts and layer everything onto the baked quiche pastry. For the filling, whisk together the eggs, pressed garlic, stripped thyme, cream, and milk and pour over the quiche.
4. Return the quiche to the oven and bake for about 30 minutes until golden brown.

Quiche au chou frisé

France

Ingrédients

- 375 g de farine
- 200 g de beurre-ramolli
- 3 cuil. à soupe d'eau
- 1 1/2 pincée de sel
- 400g de chou frisé
- 3 échalotes
- poivre noir du moulin
- 230 g de fromage râpé (Cheddar)
- 180 g de noix hachées
- 4 1/2 d'œufs
- 1 gousse d'ail
- 2 brins de thym
- 300 ml (30 cl) de crème légère
- 150 ml (15 cl) de lait

Préparation

1. Préparer une pâte brisée avec de la farine, du beurre, de l'eau et du sel et l'étaler dans un plat beurré.
2. Faire cuire la pâte au four préchauffé (200 °, th. 6) pendant 10 min. (Astuce : Pour éviter qu'elle perde sa forme, piquer la pâte avec une fourchette, y poser un papier sulfurisé, ajouter des haricots secs, les enlever après la cuisson).
3. Emincer les échalotes et mélanger avec le chou frisé préalablement cuit. Saler et poivrer. Y incorporer le Cheddar râpé et les noix et étaler le mélange sur la pâte précute.
4. Mélanger œufs, ail, thym, crème et lait et verser sur la quiche.
5. Remettre la quiche au four pour la dorer pendant 30 minutes.

Greek kale strudel

Ingredients

Filling
- 300 g potatoes
- 3 Tbsp Butaris or butter
- 400 g kale
- 2 onions
- 2 cloves of garlic
- 400 g ground beef
- salt
- 1 tsp dried oregano
- 1 tsp ground rosemary
- freshly ground pepper

Strudel pastry
- 3 packages of strudel pastry, 125 g each
- 75 g melted Butaris

Herb feta cream
- 300 g feta cheese
- 2 cloves of garlic
- 300 g plain yoghurt
- 8 Tbsp chopped herbs (e.g. dill, parsley, spring onions)

40 minutes, plus 45 minutes baking time

Tip from our kale-gourmet-team: Serve on a large wooden cutting board. Cut the strudel diagonally in pieces, spread with feta cream, and decorate with fresh herbs.

Recipe

1. Strudel: For the filling, peel the potatoes and cut into 1 cm dices. Fry them crispy at medium heat with 1 Tbsp Butaris, turning occasionally. In the meantime, remove the kale leaves, wash well, drain, and cut into large pieces.
2. Peel the onions and garlic, chop coarsely, and braise until glazed in 1 Tbsp Butaris in a large frying pan. Add the ground beef and fry for 10–12 minutes on high heat until crumbly.
3. Meanwhile preheat the oven to 180°C and place baking paper on a baking pan.
4. Blanch the kale for 3 minutes in boiling water and drain. Mix with the ground beef and season to taste with oregano, rosemary, pepper, and salt.
5. Roll out the strudel pastry, brush the surface with Butaris, and layer. Place the pastry on a floured kitchen dishtowel. Distribute the kale, meat, and potatoes as a strip along one side, leaving 5 cm free on each end.
6. Roll the strudel pastry with the help of the kitchen towel. Press the sides together to close. Place the strudel on the baking pan, brush with the remaining Butaris, and bake for 45 minutes on the middle rack in the oven.
7. Feta cream: Cut the feta cheese into small cubes. Peel the garlic and chop coarsely. Puree the yoghurt, feta, and garlic with a hand blender. Add the herbs and season to taste with pepper.

Ελληνικό στρούντελ

Greece

Υλικά

- 300 γρ. πατάτες
- 3 κ.σ. Βιτάμ
- 400 γρ. λάχανο κατσαρό πράσινο
- 2 κρεμμύδια
- 2 σκελίδες σκόρδο
- 400 γρ. κιμά
- αλάτι
- 1 κ.γ. ρίγανη
- 1 κ.γ. τριμμένο δενδρολίβανο
- φρεσκοτριμμένο πιπέρι

Σφολιάτα

- 3 συσκευασίες σφολιάτα των 125 γρ.
- 75 γρ. λιωμένο Βιτάμ

Κρέμα-τυρί φέτα με καρυκευτικά

- 300 γρ. τυρί φέτα
- 2 σκελίδες σκόρδο
- 300 γρ. φυσικό γιαούρτι
- 8 κ.σ. ψιλοκομμένα καρυκευτικά (π.χ. άνιθο, μαϊντανό, φρέσκα κρεμμυδάκια)

40 λεπτά εκτέλεση και 45 λεπτά ψήσιμο

Ιδιαίτερη ιδέα σερβιρίσματος της ομάδας-γκουρμέ-λάχανου κατσαρού:Σερβίρουμε το ρολλό πάνω σε ξυλοσανίδα. Κόβουμε το ρολλό σε πλάγιες φέτες, το επαλείφουμε με την κρέμα τυρί-φέτα και γαρνίρουμε με καρυκευτικά.

Εκτέλεση συνταγής

1. Σφολιάτα: Για τη γέμιση καθαρίζουμε πατάτες και τις κόβουμε σε κύβους 1 εκ. Τις τηγανίζουμε με Βιτάμ σε μεσαία θερμοκρασία μέχρι να ξερο-ψηθούν ολόγυρα. Στο ενδιάμεσο σχίζουμε φύ-λα από λάχανο, τα πλένουμε καλά, τα αφήνου-με να στραγγίσουν και τα χονδροκόβουμε.
2. Ξεφλουδίζουμε τα κρεμμύδια και τα σκόρδα, τα ψιλοκόβουμε σε κύβους και τα τηγανίζουμε γλ-ασσέ με 1 κ.σ. Βιτάμ σε μεγάλο τηγάνι. Προσθέ-τουμε τον κιμά και τον τηγανίζουμε σε υψηλή θερμοκρασία μεχρι να γίνει τρίμματα (10–12 λ.).
3. Ενδιάμεσα προθερμαίνουμε το φούρνο στους 180 °C και στρώνουμε μέσα σε ένα ταψί μια λαδόκολλα.
4. Ζεματίζουμε το λάχανο 3 λεπτά στο βραστό νερό και το αφήνουμε να στραγγίση. Το ανακατεύουμε με τον κιμά, και προσθέτουμε τη ρίγανη, το δενδρολίβανο, αλάτι και πιπέρι.
5. Ανοίγουμε τη σφολιάτα σε φύλλο, επαλείφο-υμε την επιφάνεια με Βιτάμ και τοποθετούμε το ένα φύλλο πάνω στο άλλο. Βάζουμε τη ζύμη πάνω σε ένα αλευρωμένο πανί. Στρώνουμε το λάχανο με τον κιμά και τις πατάτες στην άκρη κατά μήκος της ζύμης. Αφήνουμε στο κάθε άκρο 5 εκ. ελεύθερα.
6. Τυλίγουμε με βοήθεια το πανί τη ζύμη σε ρολλό. Κλείνουμε τη ζύμη στα άκρα. Τοποθετούμε το ρολλό πάνω στο ταψί με τη λαδόκολλα, τον επαλείφουμε με το υπόλοιπο Βιτάμ και τον ψήν-ουμε 45 λεπτά στο μέσο ύψος του φούρνου.
7. Κρέμα τυρί-φέτα: Κόβουμε το τυρί σε μικρούς κύ-βους. Ξεφλουδίζουμε τα σκόρδα και τα κόβουμε σε χονδρά κομματάκια. Ρίχνουμε τη γιαο-ύρτι, τη φέτα και τα σκόρδα σε ένα υψηλό δοχείο και τα κάνουμε πουρέ με μια ράβδο μπλέν-τερ. Προσ-θέτουμε τα καρυκευτικά και το ανάλ-ογο πιπέρι.

Kale pizza

Ingredients

- pizza dough for 2 baking pans
- 1 kg kale
- 2 onions
- 80 g lard
- 4 sausages (Bremer Pinkel)
- 4 pork sausages, boiled sausages, or 30 slices of cabanossi
- allspice
- pepper
- 3 cloves of garlic, chopped coarsely
- 2 tsp salt
- 1 pinch of sugar
- 2 tsp mustard
- 1/2 l water

ca. 30 minutes

Recipe

1. Prepare the pizza dough.
2. Heat up the lard in a large pot. Braise the onions until glazed. Add the kale, cook briefy, and then add the water. Grind together the salt, pepper, allspice, and garlic and add to the kale. Blend in sugar and mustard. Lay the Pinkel and pork sausages on top. Cook everything together over medium heat for 30 minutes. Taste and season again as needed.
3. The next day, roll out the pizza dough. Drain the kale over a sieve and distribute evenly over the pizza. Slice the Pinkel sausages and distribute over the pizza.
4. Cut the pork sausages into thin slices and likewise place on the pizza.
5. Preheat the oven to 220–230°C. Bake the pizza for 20 minutes.

Enjoy with a glass of cold beer – cheers!

Pizza con cavolo verde

Italy

Ingredienti

- pasta per pizza per 2 piatti di forno
- 1 kg di cavolo verde
- 2 cipolle
- 80 g di strutto di maiale
- 4 salsicce tradizionali (Bremer Pinkel)
- 4 salsicce o 30 fette di Cabanossi
- pimento
- pepe
- 3 spicchi d'aglio, in pezzi grande
- 2 cucchiaini di sale
- un po' di zucchero
- 2 cucchiaini di senape
- 1/2 l d`acqua

ca. 30 minuti

Preparazione

1. Preparare pasta per la pizza.
2. In una pentola grande far fondere lo strutto di maiale. Soffriggere la cipolla. Aggiungere il cavolo verde, lasciare cuocere un po' e aggiungere l'acqua. Tritare sale, pepe, pimento e gli spicchi d'aglio in un mortaio. Mettere tutto nella pentola. Aggiungere zucchero e senape. Aggiungere le salsicce »Pinkel« e le fette di Cabanossi. Far bollire per 30 minuti a fuoco basso. Pepare e salare.
3. Dopo un giorno allargare la pasta nel piatto di forno. Far essicare il cavolo verde in un setaccio. Spargere il cavolo verde sulla pizza. Tagliare la salsiccia »Pinkel« e condire.
4. Tagliare le salsicce o il cabanossi in fette fine e metterle sulla pizza.
5. Far prescaldare il forno a 220–230 °C. Infornare per 20 minuti.

Godere con una birra fresca. Salute!

Crostini and Chips

Roasted kale crostini

Ingredients

- 3 bunches of kale
- salt
- pepper
- bread

Recipe

1. Kale: remove leaves, wash, and cook in salted water for about 1 hour. Allow to cool in the water, then drain and chop coarsely.
2. Cut the bread into slices. Roast the slices, dip one side only into the kale water, cover with the kale, add pepper, and sprinkle with cold-pressed olive oil.

80 minutes

Kale chips

Ingredients

- 200 g kale leaves
- olive oil
- salt

Recipe

1. Remove the kale leaves from the stem.
2. Place on a baking pan, sprinkle with some olive oil and sea salt.
3. Bake for about 10 minutes at 180°C. They are ready when they're crunchy and brown but not yet black.
4. Serve with a dip. Suggestion: A light curry-yoghurt sauce complements the kale excellently.

20 minutes

Geröstete Brotscheiben mit Grünkohl (Crostini)

Germany

Zutaten

- 3 Bund Grünkohl
- Salz
- Pfeffer
- Brot

Zubereitung

1. Die Kohlblätter abstreifen, waschen und ca. 1 Stunde in gesalzenem Wasser kochen. Den Kohl im Kochwasser abkühlen lassen, ausdrücken und grob hacken.
2. Das Brot in Scheiben schneiden. Die Brotscheiben rösten, mit nur einer Seite in die Brühe des Kochwassers eintauchen, mit dem Kohl belegen, pfeffern und mit kaltgepresstem Olivenöl beträufeln.

Grünkohl-Chips

Germany

Zutaten

- 200 g Grünkohlblätter
- Olivenöl
- Salz

Zubereitung

1. Die Blätter von den Strünken abstreifen.
2. Auf ein Blech geben, mit etwas Olivenöl und Meersalz besprenkeln.
3. Bei ca. 180 Grad ca. 10 Minuten lang backen. Wenn er splittrig-crunchy und eventuell bereits braun, allerdings noch nicht schwarz ist, ist er fertig.
4. Dazu wird ein Dipp serviert. Vorschlag: Sehr gut ergänzt sich mit dem kräftigen Grünkohlgeschmack eine leichte Curry-Jogurt-Soße.

Kale with Meat and Seafood

Chinese curly kale

Ingredients

- 600 g washed kale
- 3 sticks of ginger, grated
- 3 red chili peppers, seeds removed and cut into fine strips
- 6 garlic cloves, pressed
- 3 Tbsp soy sauce
- some water
- 3 Tbsp roasted sesame seeds
- sesame oil for flavoring
- juice of a lime, alternatively some lemon juice
- 6 spring onions, cut into slices
- basic cooking oil for the wok
- 600 g tiger prawns, large shrimps

Recipe

1. Heat the oil in a wok, shortly braise the chili, garlic, spring onions, and ginger.
2. Add the washed kale and while mixing cook for at most 5 minutes until it falls apart. Meanwhile add the juice, soy sauce, and water.
3. Finally, heat the shrimps well in the vegetables and sprinkle with sesame seeds and sesame oil. During the entire cooking procedure, it is important to maintain a high temperature in the wok, so do not lower the temperature and keep stirring the contents.
4. Serve with basmati rice.

45 minutes

緑のキャベツとワサビのスープ

China

材料

緑のキャベツ　400 g

玉ねぎ　1 個

ジャガイモ　250 g

白ワイン　100 ml

コンソメスープ　300 ml

生クリーム　300 ml

ワサビ、塩、コショウ、砂糖、オリーブオイル

作り方

1．ジャガイモと玉ねぎの皮をむき、一口大に切る。鍋に入れてオリーブオイルでいためる。白ワインをふりかけ、白ワインが煮詰まったらコンソメスープを加える。

2．野菜が柔らかくなったら、生クリームを入れ、塩、砂糖、コショウで味を調える。小さくきざんだ緑のキャベツを加え、一度沸騰させる。

3．2をピューレにし、こし器でこす。

4．好みの量のワサビを入れ、味を調える。

3．2をピューレにし、こし器でこす。

Swedish Christmas kale with ham

This dish has a long tradition in the family of our local consultant: Sven Hallonsten is our Swedish hobby cook. The recipe is from the region Halland in southwest Sweden.

Ingredients

- 2 kg ham
- 5 stalks of kale
- butter
- salt
- pepper

3 hours

Recipe

1. Cook the Christmas ham for about 2 hours (occasionally adding water) and then keep it warm. Collect the meat juice and reserve for cooking kale later.
2. Wash 4–5 stalks of kale well, remove the thick stem, and chop into small pieces (or cut up in a blender).
3. Cook the kale in the meat juice for about 1 hour. Let the water boil away.
4. Then drain the kale.
5. For serving, fry the kale briefly in some butter, sprinkle with some sugar, and add enough cream until the kale takes on a soft, creamy consistency.
6. Season to taste with salt and pepper. Serve as a side dish to the Christmas ham together with other cabbages like red cabbage and brown cabbage.

Svensk julgrönkål med kokt julskinka

Sweden

Detta rätt har en lång tradition hos vår svenske hobby köksmästaren. Rezeptet kommer från Halland som ligger i Sydväst-Sverige.

Ingredienser

- 2 kg julskinka (från gris)
- 4–5 knippen grönkål
- smör
- salt
- peppar

Tillagningstid: 3 timmar

Så här lagar du julskina med grönkål

1. Lägg skinkan i en gryta och häll på med vatten så att det täcker. Koka julskinka i två timmer (fyller på lite vatten), låt sen skinkan stå i värmen.
2. Behåller spadet tills du koka grönkål
3. Skölj grönkålen (cirka 4–5 knippen) väl, ta bort grova stjälkar och hacka i mindre bitar (alt. använd mixer).
4. Koka grönkålen i skinkspadet cirka en timme. Spadet ska koka in ordentligt. Silas sen av. Vid servering bryn kålen i lite smör, strö över lite socker och tillsätt grädde för att få en mjuk konsistens. Salta och krydda efter behov. Serveras som tillbehör till julskinkan tillsammans med annan kål, som rödkål och brunkål.

Smaklig måltid!

Kale with spare ribs and candied sweet potatoes

USA

Ingredients

- 800 g fresh and washed kale
- 1 pinch of salt
- 400 g potatoes, fresh, not peeled, firm cooking
- 300 g sweet potatoes
- 100 g onions
- 1.4 kg spare ribs
- 5 Tbsp vegetable oil
- 100 g bacon
- 1 l beef stock
- 1 cinnamon stick
- 1 green pepper
- 40 g honey
- 300 ml tomato ketchup
- 2 Tbsp curry powder
- 2 Tbsp ground cumin
- 2 Tbsp ground red pepper or cayenne pepper
- 2 Tbsp soy sauce
- 2 Tbsp brown sugar

Recipe

1. Wash kale thoroughly and dry it. Boil the cabbage leaves in hot salt water for 3 minutes. Drain water from pot. Quench, drain, and press the cabbage. Dice it with a large knife.
2. Peel potatoes and put into cold water. Peel sweet potatoes, cover and keep them cool. Peel onions and dice them.
3. Cut spare ribs into portions of 3–5 ribs each. Blanch ribs in barely cooking salt water for 2–3 minutes. Remove and drain ribs.
4. Heat 3 Tbsp vegetable oil in a pot. At medium heat, sauté onions and bacon until translucent. Add kale and simmer together for another 2 minutes. Add spare ribs, water, beef stock, and cinnamon stick. Bring to a boil. At medium heat, simmer for 1 hour. Spice with salt and pepper. After 30 minutes, add potatoes, remove spare ribs, and pat them dry.
5. Whisk honey, ketchup, curry powder, ground cumin, ground red pepper, and soy sauce together. Brush thickly onto the spare ribs. Put spare ribs on a cookie tray and cook in preheated oven at 200°C for 20–25 minutes (middle rack). In the meantime, heat remaining vegetable oil in a non-stick saucepan, add sweet potatoes and fry them at medium heat for 5–6 minutes. Sprinkle with sugar and cook for about 2 minutes until light brown.
6. Remove spare ribs from the oven and serve immediately with kale and sweet potatoes.

Brasilian kale

Ingredients

- 2 kg kale
- 130 g bacon
- 2 onions
- 2 cloves of garlic
- a few drops of lemon juice

Couve is the Brasilian form of curly green kale. Thus, we have to improvise somewhat to create the typical Brasilian taste of a well-cooked cabbage.

30 minutes

A tip from our kale-gourmet-team: Sprinkle a few drops of lemon juice on the kale before serving.

Recipe

1. Wash the fresh kale under cold running water and separate the leaves from the thick stems. Then cut the leaves into 0.5 cm wide strips.
2. In a large pan, braise the chopped bacon, onions, and garlic until glazed. Add the kale and simmer for 5 minutes uncovered, check the consistency, and if necessary simmer for another 3–5 minutes. The kale needs to be tender.
3. Season with salt.

Couve à brasileira

Brasil

Ingredientes

- 2 kg de couve
- 130 g de toucinho defumado (bacon)
- 2 cebolas
- 2 dentes de alho
- 2 colheres de chá de sal
- Algumas gotas de limão

A couve é a parente brasileira do repolho crespo, é um repolho de folhas lisas. Desta forma, precisamos variar um pouco, para conseguir o típico sabor brasileiro de uma boa couve.

30 minutos

A dica especial da equipe Grünkohl-Gourmet: Antes de servir, pingue algumas gotas de limão.

Modo de preparo

1. Lavar as folhas de couve debaixo de água corrente e retirar o caule duro. Com uma faca afiada, cortar das folhas de tiras finas de 0,5 cm de largura.
2. Em uma frigideira grande fritar o bacon, a cebola e o alho cortados em quadradinhos. Juntar a couve lavada e deixar murchar por 5 minutos sem tampa. Se a couve ainda estiver dura, deixar cozinhar mais uns 3 a 5 minutos.
3. Temperar com sal.

Kale with chicken

Ingredients

- 7 Tbsp olive oil
- 6 pieces of chicken breast filet
- juice and grated peel of 1 lemon
- 6 Tbsp pine nuts
- 3 tsp each of basil, parsley, and mint
- 300 ml white wine
- 600 g white beans
- 85 ml beer
- 1.4 kg kale
- 3 cloves of garlic
- chili flakes, salt, and pepper

60 minutes

Recipe

1. Bake the chicken breasts for 2 minutes on each side in 2 Tbsp olive oil in an oven-safe pan.
2. Heat the oven at 200°C so that the meat can cook thoroughly later.
3. Prepare the marinade: Chop the basil, parsley, and mint coarsely. Press the lemon. Mix the herbs with 4 Tbsp olive oil and the juice and grated peel of one lemon. Press the garlic cloves.
4. Place the pan with the chicken in the pre-heated oven, bake for 8 minutes uncovered.
5. Heat up 1 Tbsp olive oil in a second pan. Add the garlic and chili flakes and braise briefly. Drain the white beans.
6. Add the kale to the pan with the fried garlic and heat for 1 minute. Tip: Cover the pan. The kale will cook more quickly due to the steam. Now add the white beans and pine nuts. Keep stirring to prevent burning. After 8 minutes put a cover on the pan with chicken and keep warm over low heat.
7. Now quench the vegetable pan with 85 ml beer, stir. The kale should cook for another 5 minutes. Stir often. Remove the pan from the burner when the fluid is nearly evaporated. Poultry always has to be cooked thoroughly (meat temperature 80–85°C, turkey even 90°C).
8. Add salt and pepper. Then cook the herb marinade in the pan for 1 minute with white wine. Place the chicken on a plate, cover with the white wine sauce. Serve with the vegetables – ready to eat.

Cai xoan
Vietnam

- 7 muong an dau O liu
- 6 Uc ga
- 1 trai chanh
- 6 muong an dau hat thông
- húng que, mùi tây, cây bac hà moi thu 3 nhanh
- 300 ml vang trang
- 600 g Dau tay trang (co the mua hop
- 85 ml Bia
- 1,4 kg cai xoan
- 3 tep toi
- Ot kho, muoi va tieu

60 Phut

Chuan bi

1. Uc ga rua sach roi chien moi mat 2 phut voi 2 muong dau o liu.
2. Mo lo nuong voi 200 do (de sau do nuong cho Uc ga tu tu chin).
3. Chuan bi cho phan gia vi rau: húng que, mùi tây, cây bac hà sac lon, Ep chanh lay nuoc, tat ca do vao chung voi 4 muong an o liu tron deu, toi sac nho.
4. Bo uc-ga vao 1 cai chao hoac noi va bo vao lo nuong da mo san, nuong 8 phut va nho khong can day nap.
5. Do 1 muong an dau O liu vao 1 cai chao khac, do nong, roi chien so toi va ot kho, Khui hop dau tay trang va de cho kho.
6. cai xoăn do vao cai chao co toi va ot kho va tron deu khoang 1 phut. Nho day nap de hoi nong lam cai xoăn mau chin, sau do bo dau tay trang vao cung voi hat thông, sau do tron deu tay, de khong bi chay (hay khet) bay gio 8 phut nuong ga da het, lay nap day lai va mo nho do trong lo nuong.
7. Bay gio do 85 ml Bia vao cai chao co nhung thu rau va tron deu, cai xoăn se duoc nau them 5 phut, luon luon tron deu den khi nuoc trong noi cua cai xoăn bi boc hoi it di, sau do tat lo. Uc ga phai that memm (Ga thi nuong tu 80 den 85 do nhung Ga tay thi de lo 90 do).
8. Do ruou vang trang vao cai chao co nhung thu nhu Basilim v.v. Roi nau khoang 1 phut. Sau 1 phut do la nuoc sot ruou vang trang.
9. Khi don thi bo 1 uc ga vao cai dia, do nuoc sot vang trang len va cai xoăn them vao dia, the la chung ta se co 1 phan an cai xoăn that ngon.

Spanish kale with chorizo

Ingredients

- 1 kg fresh kale
- 300 g onions
- 2 cloves of garlic
- 1 chili pepper
- 1 ring of mild chorizo
- 3 Tbsp lard

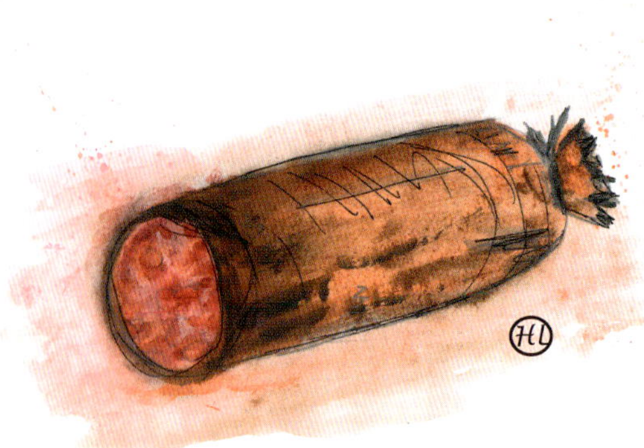

Recipe

1. Remove the kale leaves from the stems, wash thoroughly, and let drain. Blanch the kale in small portions for 2–3 minutes each in a large pot, rinse, drain, press to remove remaining water, and chop coarsely. Cut the onions into middle-sized dices. Chop the garlic finely. Cut the chili pepper in half lengthwise, remove the seeds, and cut into thin strips. Cut the chorizo into thin slices.
2. Heat the lard in a large pot. Add the onions, garlic, chili pepper, and chorizo and braise while stirring. Fold in the kale, steam briefly, and season to taste with paprika, pepper, and salt. Douse with beef broth and continue cooking at low to medium heat for 30–40 minutes with a cover.
3. Meanwhile cut a pepper in half, remove the seeds, and place it with the skin-side facing upwards on a baking pan. Grill 10–12 minutes under the preheated grill on the third rack from below, until the skin starts forming black bubbles. Cover with a moist cloth, then remove the skin and cut 2 cm large hash marks. Roast pine nuts golden brown in a pan without oil. Just before serving, place the pepper hash marks under the kale, heat, and sprinkle with pine nuts.
4. Serve with, for example, fried potato wedges.

Col Verde Española con Chorizo

Spain

Ingredientes

- 1 kg Col verde fresca
- 300 g Juliana de cebolla (la cebolla grande)
- 2 Dientes de ajo
- 1 Vaina de Pimienta Roja
- 1 Anillo de Chorizo con sabor mediano
- 3 EL Manteca
- 1 Pimineto morrón
- Piñones

Preparación

1. Separar las hojas de la col verde de su tronco, lavar cuidadodamente y dejar escurrir. La col verde en porciones se dejará en una hoya grande de 2–3 min escaldar, pasar por agua fría, dejar escurrir, exprimir y partir en trozos grandes. La cebolla será partida en cubos medianos. La vaina de pimienta roja se partirá a la mitad, se quitará las semillas y se cortará en tiras delgadas. El Chorizo se corta en rodajas delgadas.
2. La manteca se calienta en una hoya. Se agrega a cebolla, el ajo, la pimineta roja y el chorizo hasta que se ablandece todo. Recubrir la col en forma envolvente, dejar por poco tiempo que se reblandesca y sasonar con polvo de pimineta roja, pimienta y sal. Se agrega caldo de res ya preparado y con una flama media baja se deja cubierto alrededor de 45 mi. que cuesa.
3. Entretanto se parte a la mitad el pimineto morrón, se extrae el interior y con la piel hacia arriba se deja en el horno en la parte de hasta abajo. Se dejará cocer de 10–12 minutos hasta que la piel esté negra. Se cubre con un paño de tela y se quita la piel negra y se parte en rombos de alrededor 2 cm. En un sartén sin grasa se agregan los piñones y se tuestan hasta que tomen un color cobrizo. Poco antes de server se calienta el pimiento morron y la col verde y se adorna con los piñones.
4. Para acompañar se puede servir con papas fritas en gajos.

Irish stew with curly kale

Ireland

Friedrich Engels stated in Jenny Caroline Marx's autograph book that Irish Stew was his favorite dish.

Ingredients

- 1.5 kg lamb (shoulder)
- 50 g butter
- 2 onions (medium size)
- 1.5 carrots (medium size)
- 1.5 parsley roots
- 1/3 celery
- 1 kg curly kale
- 1.5 kg potatoes
- salt and pepper

ca. 40 minutes

A tip from our kale-gourmet-team:
Thyme and basil round off the flavor.

Recipe

1. Cut the meat into large square pieces.
2. Slice the onions thinly and cut the carrots, parsley roots, and celery into very thin strips (Juliennes).
3. Wash the curly kale thoroughly, let it drain, remove its leaves from the stems and quarter them.
4. Put the butter in a large saucepan, add the onions and brown them until they are golden.
5. Add the meat, brown and season it. Add water and stew it until soft.
6. Add the other vegetables and the diced potatoes, continue to stew everything until tender, season it with salt and pepper.
7. Serve piping hot in a large bowl.

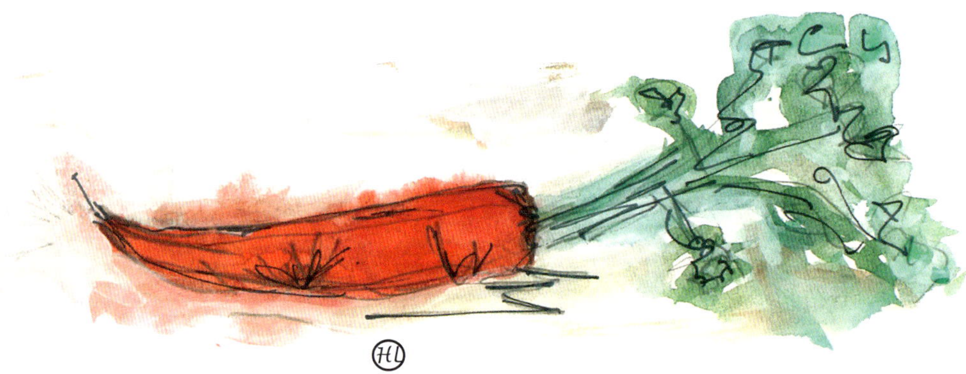

Friedrich Engels stated in Jenny Marx's autograph book that Irish Stew was his favorite dish.

Fish and Kale

Shellfish filet with kale vegetables & potato

Ingredients

- 4 portions of shellfish filet (200 g each)
- 600 g kale leaves
- 4 scallions
- 450 g potatoes
- 100 ml sweet cream
- 75 g butter
- salt, pepper, sugar, coarse mustard, mustard, nutmeg, flour, olive oil, vegetable broth

Recipe

1. Season the shellfish filets with salt and pepper and toss in flour, fry on both sides in olive oil in a non-stick frying pan, and bake for about 10 minutes at 140°C (according to the size of the filets).
2. Peel the potatoes, cut into large dices, and boil in salted water. When the potatoes are soft, drain the water and place them back into the pot and allow the remaining water to evaporate briefly. During this time, heat up the sweet cream with the butter, salt, pepper, and nutmeg. Mash the potatoes and blend in the sweet cream mixture. Season to taste with both forms of mustard.
3. Cut the kale leaves and scallions into fine strips. In a saucepan, caramelize 1 Tbsp of sugar and then throw in the kale and scallions, add some butter and vegetable broth, simmer shortly, and finally season with salt and pepper.

Schellfischfilet mit Grünkohlgemüse & Kartoffeln

Zutaten

- 4 Portionen Schellfischfilet à 200 g
- 600 g Grünkohlblätter
- 4 St. kleine Schalotten
- 450 g Kartoffeln
- 100 ml Sahne
- 75 g Butter
- Salz, Pfeffer, Zucker, grober Senf, Senf, Muskat, Mehl, Olivenöl, Gemüsebrühe

Zubereitung

1. Den Schellfisch mit Salz und Pfeffer würzen und in Mehl wälzen, von beiden Seiten anbraten und bei 140°C für ca. 10 Minuten garen (je nach Größe des Filets).
2. Die Kartoffeln schälen, in Würfel schneiden und in ausreichend gesalzenem Wasser kochen. Wenn die Kartoffeln weich sind, das Wasser abgießen und ausdampfen lassen. In der Zeit die Sahne mit der Butter, Salz, Pfeffer und Muskat aufkochen. Die Kartoffeln grob kleinstampfen und mit der Sahnemischung verrühren. Das Ganze mit den Senfsorten nach Belieben verfeinern.
3. Die Grünkohlblätter und die Schalotten in feine Streifen schneiden. In einer Pfanne einen Esslöffel Zucker karamellisieren und den Grünkohl mit den Schalotten dareingeben, etwas Butter und Gemüsebrühe hinzugeben und kurz köcheln lassen, mit Salz und Pfeffer abschmecken.

Roasted caraway catfish on kale

Ingredients

For the catfish:
- 600 g catfish filet with skin
- clarified butter
- 50 ml veal stock
- 1/2 pressed clove of garlic
- 1 tsp balsamic vinegar
- red pepper, caraway seeds, salt, pepper

For the kale:
- 250 g kale
- 50 ml white wine
- 50 ml vegetable broth
- 50 g scallions
- 40 g butter
- 40 g ham
- caraway, paprika, salt, vinegar

45 minutes

Recipe

1. Cut kale into fine strips. Melt the butter, braise the scallions, and add the kale. Braise further while constantly stirring, so that the kale turns a nice color.
2. Then add caraway, paprika, salt, ham and pepper, blend together, and quench with a few squirts of vinegar, white wine, and vegetable broth. Steam briefly. The kale should still be somewhat firm.
3. Remove the bones from the fish. To do so, cut into the skin with a sharp knife. Then fry on the skin side in clarified butter, turn and finish cooking.
4. A sauce that goes well with the dish is a paprika-caraway glaze. Season veal stock with garlic, caraway, paprika, and balsamic vinegar.
5. For a lighter variation, one can also use paprika cream sauce or whipped horseradish.

Kümmelbratl vom Wels auf Grünkohl

Germany

Zutaten

Für den Wels

- 600 g Welsfilet mit Haut
- Butterschmalz
- 50 ml Kalbsjus
- 1/2 zerdrückte Knoblauchzehe
- 1 TL Balsamicoessig
- Rosenpaprika, Kümmel, Salz, Pfeffer

Für den Grünkohl

- 250 g Grünkohl
- 50 ml Weißwein
- 50 ml Gemüsebrühe
- 50 g Schalotten
- 40 g Butter
- 40 g Speck
- Kümmel, Paprika, Salz, Weinessig

45 Minuten

Zubereitung

1. Kohl in feine Streifen schneiden. Butter zergehen lassen, Schalotten glasig anschwitzen und den Kohl dazugeben. Unter ständigem Wenden ebenfalls anschwitzen, so bekommt er eine schöne Farbe.
2. Dann Kümmel, Paprika, Salz, Pfeffer und Speck dazugeben, kurz durchschwenken und mit einigen Spritzern Weinessig, Weißwein und Gemüsebrühe aufgießen. Kurz dünsten. Der Grünkohl darf ruhig ein bisschen Biss haben.
3. Das Welsfilet schröpfen. Das heißt mit einem scharfen Messer auf der Hautseite leicht einschneiden. Dann auf der Hautseite in Butterschmalz kross braten, wenden und fertig garen.
4. Als Soße passt eine paprizierte Kümmelglace. Reduzierten Kalbsjus mit Knoblauch, Kümmel, Paprika und Balsamicoessig abschmecken.
5. Für eine leichtere Variante kann man auch Paprikaschaumsoße oder Kren-Schaum verwenden.

Ray with kale

Ingredients

- 1.2 kg ray fins
- 300 g kale
- 1 1/2 scallion
- 1 bunch of parsley
- 75 g lightly salted butter
- 1.5 l white wine
- crème fraiche
- salt
- white pepper

30 minutes

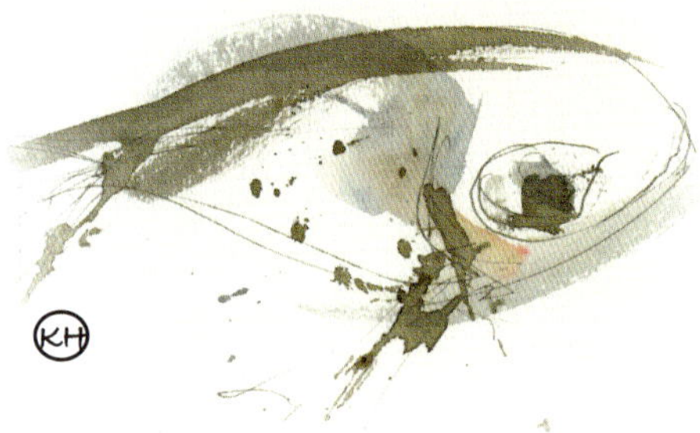

Recipe

1. Kale: Cut into strips and blanch for 10 minutes in boiling water. Drain well.
2. In the meantime clean the ray fins and remove the skin (one can also ask the fish seller to prepare the fish for cooking).
3. Smear butter generously in a gratin dish, distribute the scallion and parsley on the bottom, add the kale strips and finally add the ray fins. Quench with the white wine, distribute about 3/5 of the butter – in pieces – on the top.
4. Cook for about 10 minutes in a preheated 230°C oven.
5. Remove from the oven, spoon off 2-3 Tbsp of cooking fluid, mix with an equal amount of crème fraiche, pour onto the ray fins, distribute the remaining butter – in pieces, season with salt and pepper. Bake for a further 6–7 minutes in the 230°C oven.
6. Serve directly from the form.
7. Serve with white bread or with potatoes.

Raie au chou frisé

France

Ingrédients

- 1,2 kg (6 morceaux) d'ailes de raie
- 300 g de chou frisé
- 1 1/2 échalotes
- 1 bouquet de persil
- 75g de beurre demi-sel
- 150 cl de vin blanc
- crème fraîche
- Sel de Guérande
- Poivre blanc du moulin

30 minutes

Préparation

1. Faire bouillir une grande quantité d'eau chaude dans une marmite, puis la saler. Laver le chou frisé, l'émincer en fines lamelles et laisser cuire dans l'eau bouillante pendant 10 min. Bien les égoutter et laisser en attente sur un torchon.
2. Pendant ce temps nettoyer les ailes de raie, en retirer la peau (ou bien demander au poissonnier de les préparer).
3. Beurrer un plat allant au four et y ranger les échalotes et le persil, ensuite arranger les lamelles de chou frisé et les ailes de raie. Mouiller de vin blanc et repartir 3/5 du beurre en morceaux.
4. Glisser au four chaud (230 °, th. 7 ou 8) et laisser mijoter pendant 10 min.
5. Retirer du four, enlever 2–3 cuillerées à soupe du liquide, lier avec une quantité égale de crème fraîche, napper les ailes de raie, ajouter le beurre en morceaux, saler et poivrer. Continuer la cuisson au four pendant six ou sept minutes (230 °, th. 7 ou 8).
6. Servir dans la terrine.
7. Accompagner de pommes de terre ou du pain blanc.

Fish with onions, white wine, and cabbage

Ingredients

- 1.2 kg fish, preferably dried cod, or 4 thick filets of fish with a firm consistency
- 2 onions, cut into fine rings
- 6 Tbsp olive oil
- 1.5 kg kale
- 1.2 kg potatoes, firm cooking
- 300 ml dry white wine
- salt and pepper
- parsley, chopped
- piri-piri sauce (if desired)

ca. 45 minutes

Recipe

1. Cut the cod fish into 4 equal pieces and soak in water for 48 hours until they are bloated and completely desalted, changing the water frequently. Drain the water but do not dry the fish (remove the skin, if desired). Rinse fresh fish, salt lightly, and leave in a sieve for a few hours for the aroma to develop.
2. Preheat the oven to 180°C. Heat the oil in a large saucepan, add the onions, and sauté for 30 minutes.
3. Wash and clean the kale. Remove and place aside 4 large, well-formed leaves. Chop the remaining kale coarsely and likewise set aside. Remove the thick stems from the 4 leaves. Press the leaves flat with a wide knife and wrap the fish pieces in them. Place the packages on a baking pan and bake in the preheated oven for 20–30 minutes, until the kale leaves are dry and brown like tobacco leaves. Meanwhile pour the wine into a pot. Add the potatoes, peeled and cut into thick slices, and add enough water to cover them. Boil for 10 minutes, then add the kale. Cover well (so that the kale can steam cook) and cook until the kale is soft. Remove the potatoes and kale from the pot with a skimmer and place in a prewarmed serving dish.
4. Mix the broth with the onions in a saucepan. Season to taste with salt and pepper. Cook the sauce until it thickens. Serve by pouring the sauce over the potatoes and kale. Open the fish packages and place them on top. Sprinkle with parsley and, if desired, season with a squirt of piri-piri sauce.

Peixe com cebola, vinho branco e repolho

Portugal

Ingredientes

- 1,2 kg de peixe, preferencialmente bacalhau, mas podem ser utilizados 4 filés grossos de peixe de carne firme.
- 2 cebolas, cortadas em anéis finos
- 6 colheres de azeite de oliva
- 1,5 kg repolho
- 1,2 kg de batatas firmes
- 300 ml de vinho branco
- Sal e pimenta
- Salsinha picada
- Molho piri-piri (a gosto)

cerca de 45 minutos

Modo de fazer

1. Cortar o bacalhau em 4 pedaços grandes e deixar de molho por 48 horas até estar totalmente dessalgado. Trocar a água várias vezes. Jogar a água fora, mas não secar o peixe, retirar a pele. Salgar levemente e deixar marinar em uma peneira por algumas horas, para desenvolver o aroma.
2. Aquecer o forno a 180 °. Levar uma frigideira grande ao fogo com o azeite, juntar a cebola e deixar cozinhar por 30 minutos.
3. Lavar e limpar o repolho. Separar 4 folhas grandes e bonitas. Picar grosseiramente o resto das folhas e reservar. Retirar o caule duro das 4 folhas reservadas. Alisar as folhas com uma faca e colocar um pedaço de peixe em cada uma. Fechar como pacotes. Colocar os pacotinhos em uma assadeira e levar ao forno aquecido por 20 a 30 minutos, até as folhas de repolho secarem e terem a aparência de folhas de tabaco. Colocar o vinho branco em uma panela, juntar as batatas descascadas e cortadas em fatias grossas. Cobrir com água, temperar com sal, cozinhar por 10 minutos e juntar o repolho picado. Tampar a panela e deixar cozinhar até o repolho ficar macio. Retirar a batata e o repolho com uma escumadeira e colocar em uma travessa de servir.
4. Colocar o caldo junto com as cebolas em uma frigideira. Temperar com sal e pimenta e deixar reduzir até se tornar um molho denso. Despejar este molho sobre as batatas e o repolho. Abrir os pacotinhos de peixe e colocar por cima de tudo. Salpicar com a salsinha picada e com gotas de molho Piri-Piri.

Kale for Vegetarians

Kale with lentils

Ingredients

- 300 g lentils
- 750 g kale
- 3 chili peppers
- 6 cloves of garlic
- 1.5 Tbsp ground ginger
- 1.5 tsp basil
- 3/4 cup oil
- 2 onions, chopped finely

60 minutes

Tip from our kale-gourmet-team: Garnish with basil leaves.

Recipe

1. Select the lentils, wash, and boil until soft for about 30 minutes.
2. Remove the kale leaves, wash, chop coarsely, and boil in slightly salted water. Drain, blend the finely chopped pieces with the lentils, and press through a strainer.
3. Halve the peppers and remove the seeds. Mix with the garlic, ginger, and basil and likewise pass through a sieve.
4. Heat the oil and sauté the onions until golden. Add some water and then blend in slowly the drained ingredients. Lower the heat and simmer everything together for 15 minutes.
5. Stir occasionally and season to taste with salt.

Grünkohl mit Linsen

Germany

Zutaten

- 300 g Linsen
- 750 g Grünkohl
- 3 Peperoni
- 6 Knoblauchzehen
- 1,5 EL Ingwer gemahlen
- 1,5 TL Basilikum
- 3/4 Tasse Öl
- 2 Zwiebeln, feingehackt

60 Minuten

Der besondere Tipp des Grünkohl-Gourmet-Teams: Basilikumblätter zum Garnieren vorbereiten.

Zubereitung

1. Die Linsen verlesen, waschen und etwa 30 Minuten weichkochen.
2. Die Kohlblätter abstreifen, waschen, grob hacken und in wenig Salzwasser aufkochen. Abtropfen lassen, fein gehackt unter die Linsen mischen und passieren.
3. Die Peperoni halbieren und entkernen. Mit Knoblauch, Ingwer und Basilikum vermischen, ebenfalls passieren.
4. Öl erhitzen und die Zwiebeln darin leicht bräunen. Etwas Wasser sowie nach und nach die passierten Zutaten hinzugeben. Die Temperatur reduzieren und alles 15 Minuten schmoren.
5. Gelegentlich umrühren und mit Salz abschmecken.

Kale ravioli

Ingredients

- 600 g kale leaves
- 1 scallion
- 400 g flour
- 200 g durum wheat semolina (wheat flour)
- 8 egg yolks
- 3 egg whites
- 100 g parmesan cheese
- olive oil, salt, pepper, sugar, garlic, coarse mustard

30 minutes

Recipe

1. Prepare a noodle batter for the ravioli: Mix on the table all ingredients i.e. flour, eggs, semolina, and olive oil into a homogeneous batter, wrap in plastic foil, and store in the refrigerator for 1 hour.
2. For the filling: Braise 400 g kale leaves with the finely chopped scallion in olive oil and season with salt, pepper, sugar, and coarse mustard.
3. Then roll out the noodle batter very thinly, fill with the kale mixture, cut into squares and seal well. Then cook the ravioli in hot, salted water.
4. When the ravioli is al dente, sauté in a saucepan with a little oil 200 g coarsely chopped kale leaves and quench with a ladle of the noodle water. Transfer the ravioli to the saucepan and round out the taste of the sauce with butter and parmesan cheese.
5. Tip: The ravioli can also be frozen. After filling, just freeze for 4 hours on a pan with baking paper and then transfer to a plastic storage container. The ravioli keep well-sealed for up to 1 month.

Ravioli al cavolo verde

Italy

Ingredienti

- 600 g di cavolo verde
- 1 scalogne
- 400 g di farina
- 200 g di grana duro
- 8 tuorli
- 3 albumi
- 100 g di parmigiano
- olio d'oliva, sale, pepe, zucchero, aglio, senape di qualità crudo

circa 30 minuti

Preparazione

1. Preparare un impasto per i ravioli. Lavorare farina, uova, grana duro e olio d'oliva sul tavolo fino a quando si ottiene un impasto omogeneo. Avvolgere in pellicola alimentare e tenere in frigorifero per circa un'ora.
2. Per il ripieno: Far soffriggere 400 g di cavolo verde e una scalogna tagliata a dadi fini in un po'd'olio oliva. Aggiungere sale, pepe, zucchero e il senape.
3. Stendere la pasta riempiere con il cavolo e chiudere per bene. Cuocere i ravioli al dente in acqua salata.
4. Far soffriggere in una padella con olio d´oliva il resto del cavolo verde, tagliato in pezzi grandi. Aggiungere un mestolo del acqua di cottura.
5. Aggiungere i ravioli e condire con burro e parmigiano.
6. Consiglio: I ravioli possono essere conservati surgelati. Surgelare dopo riempito sul un piatto di forno (non si capisce) per circa 4 ore. Mettere sul piatto un po' di carta da forno. Dopo mettere in un contenitore per surgelare e ben chiuso conservare per almeno un mese.

Papas Arrugadas (wrinkled potatoes) with kale sauce

Ingredients

Sauce

- 1½ cans of tomatillos
- 5 chili peppers (fresh, large, green, mild) – poblano peppers, if available
- 2 onions
- 4½ corn tortillas (fresh or frozen)
- 6 cloves of garlic
- 200 g fresh kale
- ½ l chicken broth (for vegetarians: vegetable broth)

Potatoes

- 2 kg potatoes (small)
- 400 g sea salt

80 minutes

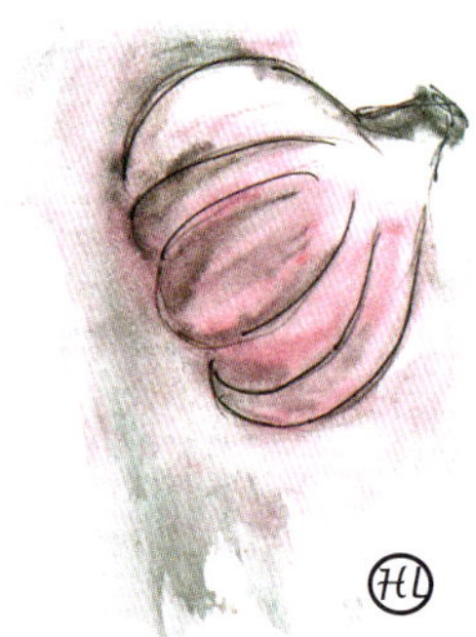

Recipe

1. Wash the kale, drain, remove the leaves.
2. Bake the chili peppers in an oven at 250°C until they develop black bubbles. Allow to cool and then peel. Halve the peppers, remove the seeds and skin inside, and chop into fine pieces.
3. Drain the tomatillos and puree with the diced onions, garlic cloves (without skin), corn tortillas, and kale.
4. Mix the puree with the chicken broth and boil for about 60 minutes.
5. Wash the potatoes well, then cook for about 30 minutes with 1.5 l water and the sea salt until done. Drain the water and place on a hot burner to allow the steam to evaporate until the peels start to wrinkle.
6. Pour the sauce with chicken broth over the potatoes.

Papas Arrugadas con Salsa de Col Verde

Spain

Ingredientes

Salsa

- 1½ Lata de Tomatillos
- 5 Chiles Poblanos grandes, frescos y de picor medianos
- 2 Cebollas frescas y sin cáscara
- 4½ Tortillas de maíz frescas o refrigeradas, dividir en pequeños pedazos
- 6 Dientes de ajo
- 200 g Col verde fresca
- 1200 ml Caldo de pollo (para vegetarianos puede ser caldo de verduras)

Papas

- 2 kg Papas (pequeñas)
- 400 g Sal de mar

80 Minutos

Preparación

1. Lavar la col verde, dejar escurrir y deshojar.
2. Asar los chiles poblanos en el horno a 250 grados hasta que se formen ampulas negras. Dejar reposar y pelar, retirar las semillas y todo el interior. Finalmente partirlos en pequeños pedazos.
3. Dejar escurrir los Tomatillos. Con todos los demás ingredientes sin el caldo de pollo mezclar y hacer un puré con la licuadora.
4. Mezclar el puré con el caldo de pollo alrededor de 60 min y dejar que hierva.
5. Lavar bien las papas, después cocer con 1,5 l. de agua y la sal aproximadamente 30 minutos hasta que estén bien cocidas. Tirar el agua y en una honilla caliente dejar que se arruge la cascara.
6. En caso de que la salsa esté muy espeza, se puede agregar caldo de pollo o de verduras.

Indian kale

Ingredients

- 1 Tbsp extra virgin olive oil
- 3 cloves of garlic
- 150 ml vegetable broth
- 1/2 tsp caraway (ground)
- 1/4 tsp Garam Masala (mixture of cloves, cardamom, pepper, cinnamon, caraway, coriander)
- 1/4 tsp salt
- 1 tsp coriander (ground)
- 1 kg kale
- 450 g chickpeas

25 minutes

Tip from our kale-gourmet-team: For those preferring it sweeter, add more cinnamon.

Recipe

1. Kale: Remove the stems and chop finely, wash well, and drain the leaves.
2. Heat up olive oil in a pot over medium heat, then add the finely chopped garlic cloves and simmer.
3. Add the kale slowly to the pot and continue cooking.
4. After about 1 minute, add all the other ingredients as well as the vegetable broth and simmer for 10 minutes over medium heat, stirring occasionally.
5. Place the chickpeas in a small boiling water bath (about 1 cup of water) and allow to absorb the water for 3 minutes.
6. Mix the chickpeas with the kale, let stand for 2 minutes, and serve.

India

भारतीय प्रकार की गोभी

आवश्यक सामग्री

1 बडा~चम्मच ज़ैतून तेल

लहसुन की 3 लौंग

150 मल सब्जी रसा

आधा चाय की चम्मच के आधे जीरा

1/4 चाय की चम्मच गरम मसाला

1/4 चाय की चम्मच नमक

चाय की चम्मच भू-धनिया

1 किलोग्राम करमसाग

450 ग्राम चिकपी

विधि

1. एक प्रकार की गोभी: अधजली दूर करना और छोटे-छोटे हैकिंग, यह अच्छी तरह धो और गिराना
2. ज़ैतून का तेल गर्मी में घट मध्यम गर्मी पर, फिर मिलाना बारीक कटे अनंतकाल और लहसुन की है-अरे! आप जाना
3. एक प्रकार की गोभी और उसके बाद के बाद तथा खाना पकाने के अंदर-बाहर
4. लगभग 1 मिनट बाद खान-पान और अन्य सभी जोड़ सब्जियां शेयर लगभग 1 मिनट बाद खान-पान और अन्य सभी जोड़ सब्जियां शेयर. 10 मिनट मध्यम गर्मी पर पकाने, सदमा पहुँचानेवाला कभी-कभार
5. चिड़िया का बच्चा मटर उबलते पानी में छोटे स्नान - पानी के लगभग 1 कप - ३ मिनट पकाना
6. एक साथ मिलकर कार्य करना और 2 मिनट पकाना

समय:

25 मिनट

विशेष छोर पर प्रकार की गोभी-टीमों के बीच:

वे लोग जिन्होंने अपने कुछ मधुर को तरजीह, हो सकता बिट अतिरिक्त दालचीनी करना होगा।

Curry and Kale in Exotic Variations

Germany

Curry and kale in imaginative variations – national dishes, crossover, fusion and innovative magical kitchens

Curry's conquest of the culinary world – leaving out the exhaustive details of these epochs – can be divided into three stages:

The leaves of the curry tree in India provided the smoky-nutty-fruity beginning. Only fresh leaves were used. India was home to exotic herb mixtures, the so-called Masalas, which became known as curry in Europe, although the mixtures varied from cook to cook. Our best-known curry powder is a British discovery, an attempt to imitate the taste of Indian dishes. Almost every curry powder includes the typical spices of the Indian subcontinent such as caraway, coriander, cloves, cinnamon, curcuma, as well as pepper, chili, and sometimes lentils.

In Germany curry was known for decades only by the finest gourmets, but then after the 1950s it became famous through the curry sausage. Curry invaded the culinary stage as a cult-condiment when the 68ers embraced new culinary horizons after a long period of self-imposed asceticism.

What the change from the »Red Star« to the cinnamon star was for Christmas cookies, the classical salt and pepper shakers gave way to the trendy curry shaker. In Peter Fischer's cookbook »Paradise – a new cookbook for societies, cooperations, poetry clubs, and other groups of people«, which was published by Wagenbach in 1975 and sold for the modest price of 3.95 DM, a cornerstone for today's gourmet world was laid with the recipe on page 126:

- 36 g coriander
- 25 g curcuma (yellow ginger)
- 25 g black pepper
- 10 g mustard seeds
- 2.5 g caraway
- 2.5 g cinnamon bark
- 5 g cardamom.

The authors of this cookbook recommend »curry handmade« according to this recipe.

Curry is a frequently used spice in multi-dish meals. It is also a popular condiment in national dishes, in the crossover and fusion kitchen, and in experimental magical kitchens.

And now let's get to kale. On the following pages you will find several innovative recipes.

Germany

Thai curry with potatoes and kale (vegetarian)

Ingredients

- waxy potatoes
- 1 onion
- 1 Tbsp canola oil
- 2 tsp homemade curry powder (or a commercial product from an Asia shop)
- 500 g kale leaves
- 1 can of coconut milk (400 ml)
- salt, pepper

Recipe

1. Peel the potatoes and cut into small dices. Cut the onions likewise into small cubes.
2. Heat 1 Tbsp oil in a pot and braise the onions until glassy. Add the potatoes and fry together briefly.
3. Blend in the curry powder, then add the kale (after boiling for 10 minutes). Blend in the coconut milk and bring to a boil. Simmer everything together in the covered pot at medium heat for about 15 minutes until the potatoes are done, stirring occasionally as needed.
4. Season to taste with salt and pepper.

Germany

»Kale curry« as a side dish for beef, ham, poultry, or fish

Ingredients

- 1.2 kg kale
- salt
- 8 onions
- 2 Tbsp olive oil
- 5 tsp homemade curry powder
- 150 g raisins
- 80 g pine nuts
- 750 ml vegetable broth
- pepper
- 2 boskop apples (red russet)

Recipe

1. Remove the kale leaves from the stems, wash, and dry well. Blanch in boiling salted water for 5 minutes, drain, and chop coarsely.
2. Cut the onions into small cubes. Melt clarified butter in a pot, braise the onions until glassy, add the curry powder, pine nuts, and raisins, and simmer together briefly. Add the kale and fill up with vegetable broth, season with salt and pepper. Simmer covered at medium temperature for 45 minutes.
3. Cut and quarter the apples, grate into the curry, and let stand.

Tip: Goes well with rice. If the kale curry is not intended as a side dish, one can add ham.

Kale curry with pork medallions

Germany

An example of the creative magical kitchen is the recipe for kale curry with pork medallions. This recipe from Martin Effenberger and Helga Frohnert won the First Prize in the Kale Recipe Competition of the Hamburger Evening News in 2006.

Ingredients

- 1.3 kg kale
- salt
- 150 g dry red lentils
- 120 g raisins
- 900 g pork fillet
- 2 onions
- 80 g lard
- 3 Tbsp mild curry powder
- 8 Tbsp mango-chutney (from a jar)
- 150 g yoghurt
- pepper
- 2 tsp sugar
- 150 ml instant chicken broth
- 1.5 cinnamon sticks (about 5 cm)

Recipe

1. Kale: wash it, remove the thick veins and stems, boil 5 minutes in salted water. Drain, collect the stock, press the kale, and chop. (To save time, one can also use kale from a jar or can.)
2. Rinse the lentils and raisins. Braise the diced onions in 20 g lard, then sprinkle with curry. Quench with 400 ml kale stock (or chicken broth). Add the lentils and cinnamon sticks and cook for 5 minutes.
3. Add the kale and cook for 20 more minutes. Remove the cinnamon sticks, blend in the raisins, 2 Tbsp (or more) mango-chutney, and yoghurt, and cook for 1 minute. Season to taste with salt, pepper, and sugar, then keep warm.
4. Cut the meat into approx. 3 cm thick slices, add pepper, and fry in the remaining lard. Add salt and mix in the remaining mango-chutney, then quench with broth. Serve the kale, meat, and sauce together.

Delicious with white wine or beer.

The Kale Classics from Northern Germany

Oldenburger kale with ham and Pinkel sausage

Ingredients

- 1.5 kg kale
- 2–3 Tbsp lard
- 4–6 boiled sausage
- 4–6 Pinkel sausage
- 250 g smoked ham
- 4 slices cured pork
- 1 tsp salt
- 1 tsp pepper
- 4 Tbsp finely chopped onions
- 1 pinch of sugar
- 3 Tbsp ground barley
- meat broth

Recipe

Kale tastes best after it has been hit by frost. One then removes the leaves from the stems, washes it thoroughly, drains it well, and blanches it with boiling water. Then it should be chopped coarsely. The onions are braised in the hot lard and then layers of kale, ground barley, and the spices are added. If necessary, add some broth. Cook everything for 10 minutes, then mix well, add the cured pork and smoked ham to the kale, cover well, and simmer over low heat for 2–3 hours. The boiled sausages and Pinkel sausages are added during the last hour. When the kale is done, the meat and sausages are removed and placed on a serving dish, and the kale seasoned once again. Serve with boiled potatoes.

Oldenburger Gröönkohl mit Speck und Pinkel

Germany

Zutaten

- 1½ kg Grünkohl
- 2–3 EL Schmalz
- 4–6 Kochwürste
- 4–6 Pinkelwürste
- 250 g geräucherter Speck
- 4 Scheiben Kasseler
- 1 TL Salz
- 1 TL gestoßener Pfeffer
- 4 EL feingehackte Zwiebeln
- 1 Prise Zucker
- 3 EL Hafergrütze
- Fleischbrühe

Zubereitung

Am besten schmeckt der Grünkohl, wenn er schon Frost bekommen hat. Man löst dann die Blätter von den Rippen ab, wäscht ihn gründlich, lässt ihn abtropfen und überbrüht den Grünkohl mit kochendem Wasser. Danach wird er grob gehackt. Die Zwiebeln werden in dem heißen Schmalz angedünstet und dann kommen schichtweise Grünkohl, Hafergrütze und die Gewürze dazu. Wenn notwendig, etwas Brühe dazugeben. Das Ganze 10 Minuten kochen lassen, dann gut durchschütteln, Kasseler und Speck zum Kohl geben und diesen fest zugedeckt 2–3 Stunden sanft schmoren lassen. Die Pinkelwürste und die Kochwürste werden erst in der letzten Stunde dazugegeben. Ist der Grünkohl gar, werden das Fleisch und die Würste herausgenommen, angerichtet und der Grünkohl noch einmal abgeschmeckt. Dazu werden Salzkartoffeln gereicht.

Bremer brown kale with Pinkel sausage

Ingredients

- 3 kg brown kale (0.5 kg brown kale is calculated for a good eater)
- 1 kg potatoes
- 40 g lard
- allspice
- salt
- pepper, ground
- 6 kale sausages
- 7 Pinkel sausages
- 5 onions
- 800 g ham (bacon)
- 800 g cured pork
- 40 g ground barley
- 2 cloves of garlic

40 minutes of preparation plus time for cooking

Tip from our kale-gourmet-team: Add 2 pressed cloves of garlic. This adds a special touch to the brown kale.

Recipe

Brown kale

1. Clean, wash, and drain the kale.
2. Heat the lard in a large pot. Peel and dice the onions and braise in the lard.
3. Add some water and then add the kale and bring to a boil in 4 steps.
4. Place the barley in hot water and allow to swell, then add the kale. Remove the skin from a Pinkel sausage and cook with the brown kale.
5. Add the ham to the pot.
6. Simmer the kale for about 2 hours over low heat. Add a pinch of allspice.
7. About 1 hour prior to serving, lay the sausages and cured pork on the kale in the pot, cover, and continue cooking.

Potatoes

Prepare either fried potatoes with ham and onions, boiled potatoes, or caramelized potatoes and serve with the hearty kale dish.

Breemsch Bruunkohl

Germany

Wat hört da to?

- 3 kg Bruunkohl
- 1 kg Kantüffels
- 40 g Swiensmolt
- Solt
- Peper
- 6 Kohlwust
- 7 Pinkelwust
- 5 Zippeln
- 200 g Swiespeck
- 800 g Kassler
- 40 g Havergrütt
- 2 Tön Knuuflook

40 Minuten för dat Torechtmaken, 3 Stunnen Kaktied.

De besünners Tipp ut de Köck: Zwee utqueschte Knuuflooktön todoon. Dodörch ward de Bruunkohl gaanz besünners aromatisch.
Nich vergeeten: För dat Fleesch ünd de Wust kümmt Semp dorto.

Wi ward dat kaakt?

Bruunkohl

1. För dat Kaken vun dan'n Kohl bruukt een bannig got Pott. Dor kummt dat Smolt rin. To dat Smolt de in lüttje Stücken sneden Zibbeln. Jümmers röhren bit de Zibbeln dörsichtig sünd.
2. Dann kümmt de tweemol waschen Bruunkohl in lüttje Etappen rin, de dörvör mit een scharp Mess lütt sneden sünd. Denn kümmt das Water rin, damit nix anbrennt.
3. De Havergrütt in springkaken Water upquellen laten ünd to dan'n Bruunkohl todoon. De maakt dan'n Kohl sämig ünd let him beten na Nött smecken.
4. Ein Pinkelwust avpellen ünd mit den kaken Bruunkohl goorn.
5. Dat dato l lekker smekt, kümmt lütt mahlen Peper, Solt rin und good röken dörchwossen Swienspeck rin. Allens good röhren.
6. Dan'n Bruunkohl lieckers 2 Stunnen op lüttje Hitt kaken. Een Kniefspitz »Wünnerpeper« (Piment) todoon.
7. Een Stünn vör'n Eten des Wust und dat Kassler op dann Kohl lengen ünd be slaaten Kackpott goorn.

Kantüffel

Kantüffel künnt as Braadkantüffel, Kakkantüffel or as karameleseerte (Braad-) Kantüffeln updischt warn.

The kale dish with syrup potatoes, created by the former East German TV cook Kurt Drummer

Kale, often also called curly kale, collards, cabbage, southern European kale, or savoy cabbage, was very popular even in former East Germany and was of course introduced on TV in all possible variations by the East German TV star cook Kurt Drummer.

Ingredients

Kale

- 6 onions
- 3/4 l meat broth
- 3 packages of frozen kale (about 600 g)
- 700 g pork belly
- 700 g cured pork
- 6 small boiled sausages

Fried potatoes with syrup

- 1.5 kg potatoes
- salt to taste
- 2 Tbsp caraway
- 60 g butter
- 3 Tbsp dark syrup

Recipe

1. Peel and dice the onions and steam in a pot with meat broth for 15 minutes.
2. Add the thawed kale and pork belly and cook for 90 minutes. After about 45 minutes, add the cured pork, 20 minutes later add the sausages and continue cooking. Season to taste with salt and pepper.
3. Boil the potatoes with salt and caraway, peel, cut into slices, and fry in butter. At the end pour the syrup over them. Stir the potatoes often.

Preparation time 20 minutes,
cooking time 90 minutes

Tip from our kale-gourmet-team:
A pinch of nutmeg rounds out the flavor.

Der Grünkohlteller mit Sirupkartoffeln, kreiert von DDR-Fernsehkoch Kurt Drummer

Grünkohl, vielfach auch Kraus-, Herz-, Welsch- oder Savoyerkohl genannt, war auch in der DDR sehr beliebt und wurde natürlich auch von Kurt Drummer, dem DDR-Starkoch, in verschiedenen Varianten im Kochstudio im Fernsehen vorgestellt.

Zutaten

Grünkohl

- 6 Zwiebeln
- 3/4 l Fleischbrühe
- 3 Packungen TK-Grünkohl (à 600 g)
- 700 g Schweinebauch
- 700 g Kasseler
- 6 kleine Kochwürste (Mettwürste)

Bratkartoffeln mit Sirup

- 1,5 kg Kartoffeln
- Salz nach Geschmack
- 2 EL Kümmel
- 60 g Butter
- 3 EL dunkler Sirup

Vorbereitung 20 Minuten, Kochen 90 Minuten.

Der besondere Tipp des Grünkohl-Gourmet-Teams: Eine Prise Muskat rundet den Geschmack ab.

Zubereitung

1. Zwiebeln schälen, würfeln und 15 Minuten im Topf mit Fleischbrühe dünsten.
2. Aufgetauten Grünkohl und Schweinebauch zufügen und 90 Minuten kochen. Nach ca. 45 Minuten Kasseler zugeben, nach 20 Minuten Würste einlegen und mitkochen. Mit Salz und Pfeffer abschmecken.
3. Kartoffeln mit Salz und Kümmel garen, schälen, in Scheiben schneiden und in Butter braten. Zum Schluss Sirup darüberlaufen lassen. Kartoffeln mehrfach wenden.

Kale Dishes Need Potatoes!

How potatoes came to Germany

Just like the key player in this book, potatoes are also immigrants. Their origin is in the Andes, a mountainous region of South America. Their path to Europe was most probably over the Canary Islands around 1570.

In Germany in the second half of the 18th century, potatoes could be found as ornamental plants in botanical gardens. Germans' taste for them was, to put it mildly, not particularly great. It was Frederick the Great who – using a legendary trick – taught them to savor now one of their favorite vegetables. He ordered potatoes to be planted in the fields and commanded his soldiers, albeit half-heartedly, to guard them. The peasants believed that it must be a very special vegetable and stole them from the fields. A perfect example of the successful integration of migrants due to the esteem of the authorities!

A brief lesson in potatoes as kale's favorite side dish

Boiled potatoes, fried potatoes, and sweet caramelized potatoes have become the most popular side dishes of kale.

There are three basic varieties of potatoes:

- Waxy potatoes
  These potatoes have a solid, fine-grained, moist consistency. They are characterized by not falling apart during cooking. Their taste includes the whole range of potato flavors, from mild to pleasantly intense. Waxy potatoes are especially suited for our favorite side dish of fried potatoes.
  Recommended types: Cilena, Nicola, Linda.

- Medium waxy
  Medium waxy potatoes have a fine-grained and somewhat moist consistency. They are characterized by tending to fall apart during cooking. These, too, have a wide variety of tastes. Medium waxy potatoes are the variety of choice for our beloved side dishes of boiled potatoes or sweet potatoes. But they are also perfect for soups.
  Recommended types: Laura, Saskia, Yukon Gold.

- Starchy potatoes
  Starchy potatoes have a coarse-grained, dry consistency. During cooking they often fall apart. Their taste is pleasantly intense. Some people prefer starchy potatoes for boiled potatoes. Their dry consistency allows them to absorb a lot of fluid, so kale broth can be nicely absorbed by the squashed starchy potatoes. They are additionally well suited for stews and mashed potatoes.
  Recommended types: Russet, Augusta, Melody.

A Little Sausage Shop

The hearty kale dishes require sausage, of course. Here »a little sausage shop« for practical use:

Bremer Pinkel

Germany

Bremer Pinkel is a Bremer classic with kale. Its main components are flare fat – the belly of pork – barley groats, onions, and spices. Its consistency is soft and it will melt on your tongue, due obviously to its high fat content.

Here is the recipe for preparing it yourself in about 40 minutes:

Ingredients

- 500 g flare fat
- 500 g barley groats
- 500 g onions
- salt
- pepper
- allspice
- pork intestine (casing)

Recipe

1. As flare fat and pork intestine are not readily obtainable, they will have to be ordered by the butcher.
2. Add the barley groats to a pot with water and a little salt and simmer until nearly cooked. We recommend this because the high fat content slows the cooking process of the groats. In the meantime, free the flare fat from the largest pieces of skin and then pass it through a grinder using a very fine blade.
3. Cut the onions into very fine dices and place them together with the ground flare fat in a bowl. Add the cool groats and season to taste with salt, pepper, and allspice. Whoever does not want to taste it raw can braise a small amount in a pan. While this tends to falsify the taste somewhat, it definitely has to be seasoned, one way or another.
4. Fill the mass into pork casing using the appropriate grinder attachment. Avoid filling it too much as the casing could burst during cooking. Form small sausages as desired. Do not separate the individual sausages from each other, as the content will spill out during cooking. Tie the ends of the sausage link and place the sausage chain in a pot of salted water. Cook the sausages for about 60 minutes.

Oldenburger Pinkel

Oldenburger Pinkel is the northwestern sister of Bremer Pinkel. The recipes are similar, except that meat is added to Oldenburger Pinkel, thus its consistency is somewhat denser.

Mettwurst

Mettwurst is a raw sausage found in innumerable variations throughout this book. Mettwurst consists primarily of pork and ham. It is preserved either by curing or by smoking.

The different types of mettwurst used in this book include the following:

- **Mettenden**
  This is a smaller and only lightly smoked variation of mettwurst. If it is not eaten with kale, mettenden can also be used in stews.
- **Brägenwurst**
  This is one of many varieties of mettwurst. What's special about brägenwurst is that a portion of pig brain is added to the mixture, although nowadays this is rarely done due to BSE considerations. This is a specialty with kale in particular in Northern Germany.
- **Lungenwurst**
  This is a specialty of northeast Germany and Denmark. A large portion of lung is added to the mixture and then seasoned. The mixture is smoked for up to two weeks in a casing. In Denmark it's eaten often on New Year's Eve.
- **Salami**
  This sausage, which is found in multiple variations in this cookbook, has a variety of regional forms. The best-known form is Italian salami. But also Hungarian paprika salami and Brazilian Salama can be found in these recipes. What they have in common is that they are for the most part air-dried. Differences are found in the length of air-drying time and in the spices used.
- **Chorizo**
  This is a Spanish paprika wurst related to salami. Chorizo consists primarily of pork and ham. It is a raw sausage seasoned with a lot of paprika and some garlic, whereas various other spices can be added according to regional preferences. The raw sausage is dried for four to six weeks and due to fermentation develops a slightly sour taste that complements its pungency well.

Bologna sausage

Bologna sausage is a boiled sausage that obtains its meaty color from the addition of pickling salt. The wurst mass is finely minced, filled into various types of casings, and finally boiled. Depending on the type, the cooked sausage might still be smoked.

Polish sausage

One can find the Polish variety of kielbasa in some of the recipes in our book. Not to be confused with the bratwurst of the same name but found extensively in Germany. Polish sausage is either dried or smoked. The pork meat found in Polish sausage is always mixed with beef.

America Discovers Kale

In the spring of 2015 the New York Times – generally considered a rather stuffy information medium – declared ecstatically: »Forget filet mignon and caviar!« The hottest dish of the day in the megacity is a humble kale salad. Restaurants were considered cool if they had a kale salad creation on their menu. Hollywood didn't want to lag behind, stars and starlets now joined the culinary hype. Kale became a superhero, it was considered the healthiest vegetable of them all. Vitamins, nutrients, calcium, and biotin – kale went sexy.

Everyone was making salad, kale chips, and green smoothies! Plastic wrapping from the supermarket became a thing of the past. Whoever wanted to be trendy and cool and thus live healthily was happy to invest the necessary dollars in shopping at the vegetable market as well as purchasing a smoothie-maker (26–27 rpm) and a kale-drying machine. Of course the kale-cutting machine for a mere $ 3,000 should also not be lacking!

To ensure that the international kale connoisseurs are not condemned to live without the recipes created by the American health freaks, we of course follow this trend and provide here a basic recipe for salads, chips, and various smoothie concoctions, which can then be varied at will.

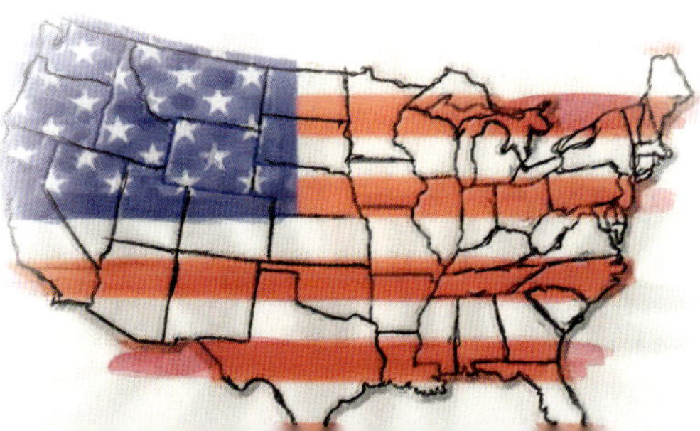

Kale salad

Ingredients

- 400 g kale
- 2 Tbsp vinegar
- 1 Tbsp lemon juice
- 2 Tbsp olive oil
- 1 tsp salt
- 3 Tbsp mustard seeds
- 1 clove of garlic
- some parmesan cheese, grated

Recipe

1. Wash the kale and cut away the thick stems. Only about 250 g of kale remain.
2. Roll the kale or press it together and chop it as finely as possible. Put it into a large bowl and blend in the vinegar, lemon juice, oil, and salt. The dense kale will soften from the vinegar and lemon juice and will slowly collapse.
3. Allow it to absorb the fluid for at least three hours, stirring occasionally. Then store overnight in the refrigerator.
4. Just before serving, braise the mustard seeds and the finely chopped garlic in oil in a saucepan. The mustard seeds can be ground in advance in a mortar mill. Blend into the kale salad.
5. While the mustard seeds are not absolutely necessary, garlic is a must. Instead of mustard seeds one can use chopped pumpkin or sunflower seeds.
6. After arranging on a serving plate, sprinkle with parmesan cheese.

Kale smoothie with pineapple

Ingredients

- 2 cups of kale, finely chopped
- 2 apples (peeled, cored, and quartered)
- 1 cup of pineapple, chopped into dices
- 1.5 cups of water

This nutritious and fiber-rich kale smoothie is a great breakfast food and, since the fruit masks the unusual kale taste, is perfect for people who don't actually like kale. Add all the ingredients to the smoothie-maker and puree to a soft, smooth consistency.

Tropical kale smoothie

Ingredients

- 1/2 grapefruit, peeled and without seeds
- 1 kiwi, peeled
- 1 ripe banana, peeled
- 2 cups of kale, finely chopped
- 2 cups of baby spinach
- 250 ml coconut milk, unsweetened

This distinctive tasting smoothie recipe is probably not for everyone. Its taste is slightly bitter, only partially compensated by the sweet fruit and coconut milk. If its flavor is too bitter, one can add some pineapple juice. Add all the ingredients to the smoothie-maker and puree thoroughly.

Kale chips

Ingredients

- 1 bunch of kale
- 1 chili pepper
- 1 cup of soaked walnuts
- 1/2 cup of yeast
- 1/2 cup of maple syrup
- 2 Tbsp lemon juice
- 1/2 Tbsp salt
- 1/2 Tbsp cayenne pepper

(1 cup corresponds to approximately one coffee mug of about 230 ml)

1. Let the walnuts incubate in the water bath overnight and then drain.
2. Mix the nuts as well as all the other ingredients – except the kale – in a mixer to a homogeneous mass.
3. Remove the kale stems, wash the leaves, and place in a bowl.
4. Add the mixture and rub the leaves with it.
5. Distribute the leaves on baking paper and bake in an oven at 80–100°C until crispy.
6. Alternatively: Dessicate in a kale-drying machine. This is the real American way!

The Cabbage Tour – from a Meeting of Dignitaries to a Common People's Winter Entertainment

Since 250 years Northern Germany celebrates a fifth season, also called the north German carnival. Between the end of November and Holy Thursday before Easter, groups pull handcarts through the countryside, toss tea bags, brooms, or balls around, and drink schnapps from the bottle. The spectacle ends with a hearty kale and Pinkel meal – usually in a rustic country inn – followed by the crowning of the king. While this certainly appears strange to outsiders, the custom has an honorable origin.

The fact is that cabbage, whether green or brown, has always been a typical northern German winter meal, in peasants' homes as well as in noble villas. The reason: kale is nutritious and healthy, resistant to frost and, beyond that, frugal, making it well suited for the barren northern soil. These attributes, however, were not responsible for its remarkable popularity in later years. Instead, it was the first »cabbage tours« or winter outings, during which cabbage was eaten since that's what was eaten in winter. This type of merrymaking, however, was clearly restricted in the middle of the 19th century to wealthy city dwellers and in addition was an exclusive privilege of men.

Let's return to Bremen. In 1848 the so-called »gate guard« was eliminated. It was no longer required to pay a gate fee when returning late to the city. There was now freedom of movement, one could stay away for any length of time. This allowed the winter outings to extend even further into the outskirts of Bremen. The procedure was always the same: After a long walk, one ate kale with smoked sausage side dishes in a rustic country inn before relaxing at a merry drinking party and a game of bowling. The local newspaper »Bremer Nachrichten« described this custom as the »golden hours in the lives of men«. These masculine cabbage tours became so popular that restaurants soon advertised discreetly.

At first, kale tours took place exclusively on Sundays, since it was a long wait until the first work-free day of Saturday. One set out in the morning, walked for a while, ate, went bowling, and returned late in the afternoon.

Interestingly, women jumped on the band wagon during these difficult times. They organized their own kale parties, despite the skepticism and mocking of their men: »Beer and cognac were not served, only strong coffee and perhaps – according to some rumors – under certain circumstances a bit of liquor … But let's not dwell on that. Gallantry has always been a masculine virtue.« Bremer Nachrichten.

World War II nearly spelled the end of this tradition. It wasn't until 1948 that restaurants again started inviting people to kale parties, in the 1950s then becoming common once again. The lean years were a thing of the past. Kale and Pinkel tours flourished and now even women were allowed to fully participate. This ushered in a significant change: Instead of bowling parties people put on their dancing feet!

Kale and Pinkel tours continue to be remarkedly popular even today. Despite all the changes over the years, the process has remained essentially the same: Hiking, eating, crowning the king. Bowling is out, instead people play bosseln or other games during the walk. CD players or DJs replace their own singing and music-making. In this the northern Germans have surpassed themselves. If you don't believe it, join a kale tour! *Helga Bürster*

Bremen

Bremen Offers More than Kale!

The residents of this lovely Hanseatic town, founded more than 1250 years ago, are proud of their independent status as one of the sixteen German States in the federal system. The heart of the city is the Market Square with its historical Town Hall built in 1648, surrounded by the Cathedral, the State Parliament, the Chamber of Commerce, and the famous **Bremen Town Musicians**.

Bremen operates the second most important harbor in Germany, although in the city this is hardly noticed, since the main port is located in Bremerhaven. The State is composed of the very traditional Hanseatic town of Bremen and maritime city of Bremerhaven, where even the largest container ships can be accommodated along the five kilometer (!) long riverside quay. This is also where the busy cruise ship terminal is located and the many unique and unusual museums and multimedia German Emigration Center can be visited.

Also noteworthy are world's largest Mercedes plant, the steel mill, Beck's Brewery, well known shipyards and shipping companies, the Airbus and Space Industry, shipbrokers, the film industry, multiple universities and many hidden champions.

»Bremen is a beautiful cosmopolitan city« say the inhabitants. Here you can live well, a green city with lovely neighborhoods. A metropolis of bicyclists, short distances, WERDER BREMEN the successful football team, and the singular drop tower. All the cultural sights and historical attractions can be reached by foot. It's a pleasure to stroll along the

Old Bremen Harbor

meandering city streets and diverse shopping malls, to dine in the noble or small, quaint restaurants, or to visit the trendy bars and taverns.

The Ostertor-Quarter, characterized by tiny winding streets, offers amazing impressions and insights. It is always worthwhile to just roam through its numerous streets with their typical picturesque **Old Bremen Houses**, most of which were built around 150 years ago.

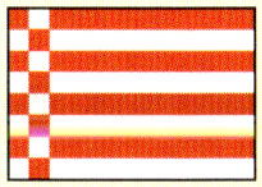

The Free Hanseatic Town of Bremen extends more than 42 km along the River Weser, about 50 km from the north sea, traversed by more than 700 km of bike paths on an area of 420 square kilometers. This smallest German State comprises the towns of **Bremen and Bremerhaven** with a total of 680,000 inhabitants. About 565,000 people live in Bremen. The state coat of arms displays the key of Bremen.

The Bremen State Parliament (Bürgerschaft) is the citizens' representation and is elected every four years. The State Government of Bremen consists of Senators (Minister). The President of the Senate is also the Mayor of Bremen. The Town Hall is the seat of the State Government.

www.bremen.de

Old Bremen Houses

The marvellous Market Square of the kale metropole

Bremer Stadtmusikanten (the Bremen Town Musicians sculpture) was created by Gerhard Marcks in 1953 and is probably the most popular sculpture of these fairy tale figures.

The Rathaus (Town Hall) was erected from 1405–1410. The splendid façade was created by Lüder von Bentheim and finished 1648. The oldest part of the Town Hall the Ratskeller (wine cellar) was built 1408 due to the city council's monopoly on wine. Only German wines are served there. The magnificent carved wine casks are for decoration only. The restaurant offers typical North German home-style cooking, including kale in winter months, of course.

The Obere Rathaushalle (Upper Hall) was in early centuries a celebration and reception hall but also a conference hall for the town council. When entering the hall you will feel its solemn dignity. The outer building, the so-called Neues Rathaus (New Town Hall), built from 1909–1913.

Opposite the Town Hall is the **House of Parliament** (Bürgerschaft), erected 1964–1966, and the **Schütting**. It is the guild house for Bremen's Chamber of Commerce. Built 1537–1538, it was enlarged by gables and a balustrade in 1594.

Schütting

The 10 meter tall statue of **Roland** was made in stone in 1404 after the archbishop's servants had burned the wooden precursor. The Roland statue symbolises the self-confidence of Bremen's citizens.

The St.-Petri-Dom (cathedral) is one of the oldest cathedrals in Germany and was erected in its present form between 1035 and 1072. After subsequent rebuilding the cathedral shows elements of late Gothic and late Romanesque periods. In the 19th century the towers were restored.

Near the Market Square is the **Böttcherstraße** with the most impressive and outstanding red brick-lined architecture, as well as the daily glockenspiel (chimes) with carved wooden panels, in memory of the first successful flight from Bremen to Canada in 1927. The original plane BREMEN is displayed in the Bremen airport.

Böttcherstraße

The **Schnoor Quartier** contains the oldest houses dating back to the 15th and 16th centuries. Nowadays, countless artists and craftsmen live in this idyllic district. Besides numerous interesting and inviting handcraft shops you'll also find small antique shops, quaint galleries, nice renowned pubs and many good restaurants. *Klaus Kellner*